Effective Motivation

Developing Management Skills

Developing Management Skills

EFFECTIVE MOTIVATION

David A Whetten
Kim Cameron
Mike Woods

HarperCollins*Publishers*

Adaptation published by arrangement with HarperCollins Publishers, Inc, USA.

This edition first published in 1996 by
HarperCollins College
An imprint of HarperCollins Publishers Ltd, UK
77-85 Fulham Palace Road
Hammersmith
London W6 8JB

British Library Cataloguing in Publication Data. A catalogue record for this book is available from the British Library.

ISBN 0-00-499041-2

Typeset by Dorchester Typesetting Group Ltd
Printed and bound by Scotprint Ltd, Musselburgh
Cover design: The Senate

Other Titles in the Series

Effective Conflict Management
Effective Problem-Solving
Effective Communication
Effective Empowerment and Delegation
Effective Stress Management

Contents

Preface

Effective Motivation is one of a series of six books based on *Developing Management Skills for Europe*, a major work by David Whetton, Kim Cameron and Mike Woods. The other titles from this series are *Effective Stress Management, Effective Problem-Solving, Effective Communication, Effective Conflict Management* and *Effective Empowerment and Delegation*. Presented in a convenient form they provide a background of reading and exercises for tutors and students taking MBA grade or other business qualifications.

Each book in the series seeks to find a balance between a sound theoretical background and case studies. Our objective remains, as it did in the combined work, to develop behavioural skills not only to increase knowledge and understanding in the area, but also to enable readers to apply what they have learned. We hope our readers will be able to achieve their qualifications and to become productive members of their organisations by learning applicable skills.

The structure of the books and the method of teaching they employ are, in our opinion unique. Each book begins with a series of questionnaires designed to check on the reader's present understanding of the area, and in some cases assist the reader in self assessment. Thus, in the present book, *Effective Motivation*, the reader is asked to consider his or her state of knowledge in the area of motivation.

From these questionnaires the reader will be able to set learning objectives for the book, and on finishing the text see how much he or she has been able to relate to the very personal world of self.

The main body of the text provides a background to the issues of motivating others, why it is important, and what and how it can be improved. The text closes with case studies, discussion questions, exercises and a section on Application Planning.

Our firm belief is that when 'all is said and done, there is more said than done'. We are asking our readers to make a real commitment to use the material and become more effective in their chosen professions.

Introduction

John Syer, sports psychologist (1986), describes the most difficult problem a football manager has to face. It is when talented players are not giving their best. As football is essentially a team game, it's not so easy to see when a talented player lets go of the ball a fraction too early to avoid a potentially damaging tackle or hesitates very, very slightly before tackling another player himself. In the language of the sports field, the player lacks motivation and it is the job of the captain, the support staff, the rest of the team and most of all the player himself, to regain that motivation. Without the motivation of all the players, team spirit fails and the team loses. Football management is merely one area of management and its problems with motivation are universal.

> A large pilot plant to make smokeless fuel was operating in the British Midlands coal fields. In the process, air was forced into powdered coal by a massive fan. If the fan failed the whole plant would be at risk.
>
> Just before the change over to the night shift, the plant stopped. All the emergency procedures were initiated and the team managed a safe shut-down. At the end of the shut-down operation a shift operator who was due on the next shift appeared. He was very concerned and rather frightened. He had been passing the fan room on his way to sign in when he heard a rather strange noise. He was not normally allowed into the fan room but he went in all the same and heard the strange noise close up – he thought it was the main bearing of the main fan and he pressed the emergency button to stop the whole plant. In pressing the button he saved a very costly accident. He was not certain that he had done the right thing and was surprised to be thanked formally by the Plant Manager for his prompt action.

The process worker could well have ignored the noise, the fan would have seized up and the team, in the sporting analogy, would have failed. The fan was not the process worker's direct responsibility but he was *motivated* to act beyond his immediate area of work. Handy, in his book, *The Age of Unreason*, sees a time when we will all have to accept what he calls the 'inverted doughnut' job description. Unlike a normal doughnut it is the inside that is solid – our core job, and the outside that is the 'hole' – a fuzzy area of responsibilities. For many of us it is the fuzzy outside area wherein our motivation lies. The core of the process worker's job was to attend the control room of the plant over a particular shift pattern and to watch a number of instruments. The fuzzy part of his job was concerned with the total function of his team. To work in this area, with the attendant risks, requires personal motivation, good and concerned communication from his manager and the support of the team. Communications, trust and support are the keys to motivation and are the basis of this book. We make no apology for what may be seen as a rather tough approach – management is, in most cases, about getting things done effectively and we might say hesitatingly – at a profit. It's a tough world.

Skill Pre-assessment

Diagnostic Surveys for Motivating Others

Instructions

Step 1: Before you read the material in this book, please respond to the following statements by writing a number from the rating scale below in the left-hand column (Pre-assessment). Your answers should reflect your attitudes and behaviour as they are now, not as you would like them to be. Be honest. The instrument is designed to help discover your own level of competency in motivating others so you can tailor your learning to your specific needs. The Scoring Key, which will help you to identify the areas of the book most important to you, is at the end of the book, page 83.

Step 2: After you have completed the reading and the exercises in this book and as many of the Skill Application assignments as possible, cover up your first set of answers. Then respond to the same statements again, this time in the right-hand column (Post-assessment). When you have completed the survey, check out your scores using the Scoring Key at the end of the book to measure your progress (page 83). If your score remains low in specific skill areas, use the behavioural guidelines at the end of the Skill Learning section (page 57) to guide further practice.

Rating Scale

6 Strongly agree	5 Agree	4 Slightly agree
3 Slightly disagree	2 Disagree	1 Strongly disagree

ASSESSMENT

PRE- **POST-** **Imagine that you are supervising the work of a subordinate.**

_____ _____ 1. If there is a problem of work being done badly or inefficiently the first thing I would do is to check whether the worker had the skills, knowledge and tools to do the job, then I would worry about motivation.

_____ _____ 2. I would establish the standards I expect the subordinate to achieve.

_____ _____ 3. If necessary I would offer to provide training and would not take over the job myself.

_____ _____ 4. I would be straightforward in providing feedback of how he/she is doing and what his/her chances are of moving up in the organisation.

_____ _____ 5. I always attempt to find ways of rewarding exceptional performances.

_____ _____ 6. If it came to having to discipline the subordinate I would identify the problem, describe its consequences and explain how it should be corrected.

_____ _____ 7. I try to make work both interesting and challenging.

_____ _____ 8. I try to match the rewards to the person when the job is well done.

_____ _____ 9. I make sure that the person feels fairly and equitably treated.

_____ _____ 10. I make sure that the person gets timely feedback from those affected by task performance.

_____ _____ 11. I attempt to find the reasons for poor performance before taking any remedial or disciplinary actions.

_____ _____ 12. I always help the person to set targets that are challenging, specific and time-bound.

_____ _____ 13. Only as a last resort do I attempt to move or fire anyone.

_____ _____ 14. Whenever possible I make sure valued rewards are linked to high performance.

_____ _____ 15. I am very tough when the effort is below what is required and I know what can be achieved.

_____ _____ 16. I try to make work more interesting by moving people to other jobs and by modifying jobs so that there is variety.

_____ _____ 17. I try to arrange for team-working wherever possible.

_____ _____ 18. I make sure that any judgements of performance are fair.

_____ _____ 19. I reward success immediately.

_____ _____ 20. I always determine if the person has the necessary resources and support to succeed in the task.

Work Performance Assessment

Instructions

Respond to the following statements, based on your current (or recent) work situation. Then turn to the end of the book for the Scoring Key (page 84).

Rating Scale

5 Strongly agree	**4** Agree	**3** Neutral
2 Disagree	**1** Strongly disagree	

Imagine that you are being supervised in a job.

1.	My supervisor and I agree on the quality of my performance.	1 2 3 4 5
2.	I feel I have adequate training to perform my current job assignments.	1 2 3 4 5
3.	I believe that my natural skills and abilities are matched very well with my job responsibilities.	1 2 3 4 5
4.	I believe that I have adequate resources and supplies to do my job well.	1 2 3 4 5
5.	I understand my boss's expectations and generally feel they are realistic.	1 2 3 4 5
6.	I believe that rewards are distributed fairly, on the basis of performance.	1 2 3 4 5
7.	The rewards and opportunities available to me if I perform well are attractive to me personally.	1 2 3 4 5
8.	My supervisor says I am not performing as well as I should, but I disagree.	1 2 3 4 5
9.	I could do a much better job if I had more training.	1 2 3 4 5
10.	I believe that my job is too difficult for my ability level.	1 2 3 4 5
11.	I believe that my job performance is hindered by a lack of resources.	1 2 3 4 5
12.	I believe my boss's expectations are unclear and pretty unrealistic.	1 2 3 4 5
13.	I believe my boss prefers favourites when allocating rewards.	1 2 3 4 5
14.	I do not find the rewards and opportunities available to high performers very appealing.	1 2 3 4 5

Skill Learning

Increasing Motivation and Performance

> 'I can't understand why we have such bad luck with Directors of Engineering. Our first head of engineering was technically well qualified. He'd been a good designer for us before we promoted him. But he started drinking heavily, and he had to go. We replaced him with Harris who seemed so promising. They say he is doing well in his new job at the Beta Company. But they operate differently to us. Then we appointed Steve Spencer and he seemed to have all the qualifications we needed. And he certainly was a gentleman. But he never could get things done. Apparently he couldn't gain the respect of the design team. So, here we are, looking for another replacement. I'm beginning to wonder whether we'll ever find the right one.'
>
> Source: Dalton, Lawrence and Lorsch, 1970.

This is how a well developed case study, 'Higgins Equipment Company', closes. The comments of the company chairman reflect the frustration he had experienced in trying to staff a key post. He had filled the position three times with individuals of experience and high promise, but their performance was consistently disappointing. The case details several structural obstacles facing any occupant of the job:

- Several sub-units in the engineering division perform production and marketing activities.
- The director is both the head of engineering and the director of a sub-unit called Engineering Services, which co-ordinates engineering and production activities.
- One of the department heads in engineering has informal direct access to the president.

A problem that was initially seen as one of motivation, turns out to be much more fundamental.

Diagnosing Work-Performance Problems

Unfortunately, many managers share the bewilderment of the manager in the case study. His approach brings to mind the Chinese proverb, 'For every hundred men hacking away at the leaves of a diseased tree, only one man stoops to inspect the roots'. The purpose of this book is to examine the analytical and behavioural skills that are missing in the Higgins case. The first part of this book examines how to identify the underlying causes of performance problems. The second part presents a six-step process for creating a highly motivating work environment.

We need a model to guide the inquiry process. Maier (1973) and Lawler (1973) have summarised the determinants of task performance as follows:

$$\text{Performance} = \text{Ability} \times \text{Motivation (Effort)}$$
$$\text{Ability} = \text{Aptitude} \times \text{Training} \times \text{Resources}$$
$$\text{Motivation} = \text{Desire} \times \text{Commitment}$$

According to these formulae, **performance** is the product of ability multiplied by motivation, and **ability** is the product of aptitude multiplied by training and resources. The fact that there is multiplication in these formulae suggests that all elements are essential. For example, workers who have 100 per cent of the motivation and 75 per cent of the ability required to perform a task can perform at an above-average rate. However, if these individuals have only ten per cent of the ability required, no amount of motivation will enable them to perform satisfactorily.

Aptitude refers to the inherent skills and abilities a person brings to the job. These obviously involve physical and mental capabilities. But for a job where the people factors are paramount, they also include personality characteristics. Most of our inherent abilities can be enhanced by education and training. Indeed, much of what we call native ability in adults can be traced to previous experiences of developed skills, perhaps by informal contacts – modelling the social skills of parents or older siblings. Nevertheless, it is useful to consider training as a separate component of ability, since it represents an important mechanism for improving employee performance. When we are attempting to match people to jobs in any selection process ability should be matched to the skill requirements of the job. If an applicant has minor deficiencies in skill aptitude but many other desirable characteristics, an intensive training programme can increase the applicant's qualifications to perform the job (Wanous, 1980).

Motivating Others

Our definition of ability is broad. We are focusing on the ability to perform, rather than the ability of the performer. Frequently, highly capable and well-trained individuals are placed in situations that inhibit job performance. Specifically, they are not given the resources (technical, personnel, political) to effectively perform assigned tasks.

Motivation represents an employee's desire and commitment, and is recognised as effort. Some people want to complete a task but are easily distracted or discouraged. They have high desire but low commitment. Others continue with impressive persistence, but their work is uninspired. These people have high commitment but low desire.

The first question that must be asked by the manager of a poor performer is whether the problem stems from lack of ability or lack of motivation. Ask the question 'CAN he or she do what is required?' before asking 'Does he or she WANT to do it?' There are four pieces of information that managers need in order to answer this question (Michener, Fleishman and Vaske, 1976):

1. The difficulty of the tasks assigned to the individual.
2. The known ability of the individual.
3. The extent to which the individual seems to be attempting to perform.
4. The degree to which the individual's performance improves with coaching (see the book in the series – *Effective Communication*).

Low ability is generally associated with very difficult tasks, overall low individual ability, evidence of strong effort and lack of improvement over time.

The answer to 'Is this an ability or motivational problem?' has far-reaching ramifications for manager–subordinate relations. Managers tend to become forceful if they believe that an individual is deliberately not doing what is requested and has no justifiable excuse. Managers justify their choice of action on the grounds that the subordinate has a 'poor attitude', is hostile to authority or lacks dedication (Kipnis, 1976).

Unfortunately, if the manager's assessment is incorrect and poor performance is related to ability rather than motivation, the response of increased pressure will make the problem worse. If poor performers feel that management is insensitive to their problems – that they lack resources, are inadequately trained or are forced into unrealistic time schedules – they may respond in a counter-productive manner to any tactics aimed at increasing their effort. They are likely to develop a motivational problem – their desire and commitment will decrease in response to management's insensitive, dictatorial behaviour. Seeing this response, management will feel that their original diagnosis is confirmed and they will proceed to use even stronger forms of influence to force compliance. The resulting vicious circle is extremely difficult to break and emphasises the dangers in faulty analysis of performance problems.

In the remainder of this book, we will examine the two components of performance in more detail. We will discuss manifestations of low ability and poor motivation, their cases and some proposed remedies. Overall, we will devote more time to motivation. While ability tends to remain stable over long periods of time, motivation fluctuates; therefore, it requires closer monitoring and frequent recharging.

Enhancing An Individual's Ability

Our problem-solving performance should be based on the principle of Ocham's Razor:

> When you have eliminated all the obvious solutions from a problem, what remains, however unlikely, is the cause.

In our case 'lack of ability' covers what we see as the obvious solution and motivation, 'however unlikely' is only discussed when these have been eliminated.

Lack of relevant abilities to do a job effectively may come from several causes:

- The resources necessary for the job may not be available
- Ability may have been improperly assessed during the selection process
- The technical requirements of a job may have radically changed
- The person who performed very well in one post may be promoted to a higher-level position that is too demanding (the so-called Peter Principle where people are typically promoted to one grade above their level of competence)

The first cause – the lack of relevant resources, must be disposed of before we proceed with the others. This process may involve all the communication skills at our disposal. The skilled manager may note that 'lack of relevant resources' is really a criticism of him or her, and may well want to remove this first as 'a wise career move'.

Having resolved the 'material' problems, we need to look at the personal issues, and managers should be ready to look at the symptoms of failing personal performance. There are three danger signals which can be recognised in failing subordinates (Quick, 1977):

1. **Taking refuge in a speciality.** Managers or supervisors lose their ability to manage and retreat to their technical speciality. This often occurs in general managers who feel insecure addressing problems outside their area of expertise and experience. Anthony Jay, in *Management and Machiavelli* (1967), calls this type of manager a 'George I', who, after assuming the English throne, continued to be preoccupied with the affairs of his native Hanover in Germany.
2. **Focusing on past performance.** Another sign is measuring one's value to the organisation in terms of past performance or on the basis of former standards. Some cavalry commanders in the First World War relied on their outmoded military knowledge and as a result failed miserably in mechanised combat. This form of obsolescence is common in organisations that

fail to shift their mission in response to changing market conditions.

3. **Exaggerating aspects of the leadership role.** Managers who have lost confidence in their ability tend to be very defensive. This often leads them to exaggerate one aspect of their managerial role. Such managers might delegate most of their responsibilities because they no longer feel competent or they may reduce their role to that of an administrator whose sole aim is to scrutinise every detail. Others become devil's advocates. Their negative approach doesn't stimulate creativity and indeed thwarts efforts towards any change.

Remedies for Failing Performance due to Lack of Ability

To begin with, once a manager has ascertained that lack of ability is the primary cause of poor performance, a performance review interview should be scheduled.

There are five principal tools available for overcoming poor performance problems due to lack of ability which we will call:

- Refurbish
- Retrain
- Redeploy
- Reassign
- Release

We will discuss these in the order they should be considered by a manager.

Unless the manager has overwhelming evidence that the problem stems from low aptitude, it is wise to initially assume that it is due to a lack of resources or training. This gives the subordinate the benefit of the doubt and reduces the likely defensive reaction to an assessment of inadequate aptitude.

The **refurbish** option focuses on the support needs of the job, including personnel, budget and political clout. Asking, 'Do you have what you need to perform this job satisfactorily?' allows the subordinate to express his or her frustration over inadequate support. Managers should be cautioned that poorly-performing subordinates typically blame external causes (Snyder, Stephen and Rosenfield, 1978; Staw, McKechnie and Puffer, 1983). One should investigate the subordinate's complaints about lack of support in detail to determine their validity. But even if employees exaggerate their claims, starting your discussion of poor performance in this manner signals your willingness to help them solve the problem from their perspective. The techniques and style of the discussions are detailed in the book from the series – *Effective Communication*.

Retraining is the next option to consider. The need for a continuous upgrading of skills is vital in rapidly changing work. Training programmes can take a variety of forms. For example, many firms are using computer technology more in education. This can involve interactive technical instruction and business games that simulate problems likely to be experienced by managers in the organisation. More traditional forms of training include subsidised external courses and in-house technical or management seminars. Some companies have experimented with company sabbaticals to release managers or technical specialists from the pressure of their work so they can concentrate on retraining. It is becoming more common for large organisations – the BBC, Allied Domecq – to sponsor their managers to take MBA programmes. General Motors in the UK, along with many other organisations have established a 'learning facility' in the Luton site open to all employees (and now the citizens of the area), where individuals can learn at their own pace subjects of their own choice. Retraining is becoming a continuous process and part of the new ideal – the 'Learning Organisation'.

If re-supplying and retraining are insufficient remedies for poor performance, the next step should be an attempt to **redeploy**. The employee maintains his or her position while the various components of the work are analysed. Once the job has been explored as a process it can be seen whether the particular employee can contribute to the accomplishment of the same task in some restructured form. For example, an assistant may be brought in to handle many of the technical details of a first-line supervisor's position, allowing more time for the supervisor to focus on people development or to develop a long-term plan to present to upper management.

If a revised job description is unworkable or inadequate, the fourth alternative is to **reassign** the poor performer – to find new jobs more suited for individual capabilities. This may be, and often is, a position of less responsibility or to one requiring less technical knowledge or interpersonal skills. For example, a medical specialist in a hospital who finds it increasingly difficult to keep abreast of new medical procedures but has demonstrated management skills might be shifted to a full-time administrative position.

The last option is **releasing**. If retraining and creative redefinition of the task has not worked and there are no opportunities for reassignment in the organisation, releasing the employee from the organisation should be considered. This option may well be outside the immediate superior's responsibility and constrained by union agreements or company policies, but all too often chronic poor performers who could be released are not, because management chooses to side-step a potentially unpleasant task. Instead these individuals are put 'on the shelf', out of the mainstream of activities, where it is perceived that they can't cause any problems. Even when this action is motivated by humanitarian concerns ('I don't think he could cope with being sacked'), it often produces the opposite effect to that desired. Actions taken to protect an unproductive employee from the embarrassment of dismissal just substitute it with the humiliation of being ignored. Obviously, dismissal is a drastic action that should not be taken lightly. However, the consequences for the unproductive individuals and their co-workers of allowing them to remain after everything else has been tried, should be weighed carefully. It is in the interest of both the company and the individual that if nothing else is possible, he or she is encouraged to do something new with their lives.

Fostering a Motivating Work Environment

Once we have considered the above, we can move on to the issues of motivation. Effective managers devote considerable time in gauging and improving their subordinates' motivation. The tragedy of the Higgins case is the inability of the company chairman to diagnose the real reasons for the poor performance of the directors of engineering. He ignored the structural problems and attributed the repeated failures to inadequacies in those occupying the position. No matter how well-qualified and highly motivated Steve Spencer's replacement, it is likely that he or she will also be judged incompetent.

In a major contribution to management thinking, Douglas McGregor (1960) labelled a focus on the incompetence of workers as 'Theory X'. The basic assumption of Theory X is that people really do not want to work hard or assume responsibility. Accepting this assumption the job of a manager is reduced to that of someone who coerces, intimidates, manipulates and supervises. McGregor provides an alternative set of assumptions, which he terms 'Theory Y'. In Theory Y employees want to do a good job and assume more responsibility. Management's role is thus to enable workers to reach their potential by productively channelling their motivation to succeed. Unfortunately, McGregor believed most managers subscribe to Theory X assumptions about workers' motives.

The alleged prevalence of the Theory X view brings up an interesting series of questions about motivation:

- What is the purpose of teaching motivation skills to managers?
- Should managers learn these skills so they can help employees reach their potential?
- Are we teaching these skills to managers so they can more effectively influence their employees' behaviour?

These questions naturally lead to a broader set of issues regarding employee–management relations. Assuming a manager feels responsible for maintaining a given level of productivity, is it also possible to be concerned about the needs and desires of employees? In other words, are concerns about employee morale and company productivity compatible, or are they mutually exclusive?

Contemporary research combined with training programmes (Greene, 1972; Levering, Moskovitz and Katz, 1984) support the position that concerns about morale and performance can coexist.

		EMPHASIS ON PERFORMANCE	
		Low	High
EMPHASIS ON SATISFACTION	High	Indulging	Integrating
	Low	Ignoring	Imposing

FIGURE 1 Relationship between satisfaction and performance

As shown in Figure 1, effective motivational programmes not only can but must focus on increasing both satisfaction and productivity.

A high emphasis on satisfaction with a low emphasis on performance represents an irresponsible view of the role of management. Managers have the job of making their organisations run effectively and measuring individual performance is part of that job. Managers who emphasise satisfaction to the exclusion of performance will be seen as nice people, but their management style undermines the respect of their subordinates. It is easy to imagine an organisational climate that is so focused to the goal of satisfaction that management becomes dominated by the needs of employees and the resulting club-like atmosphere hinders good performance.

A strong emphasis on performance to the exclusion of satisfaction is equally ineffective. This time instead of indulging, the manager is imposing. There is little concern for how employees feel about their jobs. The boss gives the orders and the employees must follow them. Employees who feel expolited are unhappy employees, and as Peter Herriot and Carole Pemberton (1995) state, they have three strategies open to them:

- Get out
- Get safe
- Get even.

None of these are satisfactory outcomes for an organisation. While exploitation may increase productivity in the short run, its long-term effects generally decrease productivity through increased absenteeism, employee turnover, and in some cases, even sabotage and violence.

When managers emphasise neither satisfaction nor performance, they are ignoring their responsibilities. There is no real leadership, in the sense that employees are given neither priorities nor direction. Paralysed between what they consider to be mutually exclusive options of emphasising performance or satisfaction, managers choose neither. The resulting neglect, if allowed to continue, may ultimately lead to the failure of the unit for which the manager has responsibility.

An integrated approach emphasises performance and satisfaction in balance. Instead of accepting the conventional wisdom that says competing forces cancel each other out, enterprising managers capitalise on the tension between the combined elements and forge new approaches. However, this does not mean that both objectives can be fully satisfied every time. Some trade-offs occur naturally in certain situations – but in the long run, both should be given equal consideration.

The integrated view of motivation proposes that while sustaining employee morale is important, it should not overshadow management's responsibility to hold people accountable for results. Managers should avoid the twin traps of working to engender high employee morale for its own sake or pushing for short-term results at the expense of long-term commitment. The best managers have productive people who are also satisfied with their work environment (Nadler and Lawler, 1977; Jordan, 1986).

This view of management is reflected in David Bradford and Allan Cohen's management guide, *Managing for Excellence* (1984, p. 21). 'Excellence requires budget and control systems, formalised ways to appraise, reward and promote long-range planning and forecasting systems, and division of labour and job descriptions. The dilemma for the manager, then, is not whether control needs to be exercised, but how to see that it is exercised without weakening the motivation of those with energy and enthusiasm'.

Hersey and Blanchard (1982) contend that organisational success and performance is affected by the congruence between the objectives of the managers and those of their subordinates. They argue that the organisation can only accomplish its objectives if those of the managers and subordinates are supportive of each other and the organisation. As a result managers need to adjust their style to meet the needs of their subordinates. These needs are measured in terms of their psychological maturity. As maturity develops and subordinates are increasingly willing and able to accept greater responsibility, the manager's style changes from telling to selling to participating, and finally to delegation.

Elements of an Integrated Motivation Policy

The purpose of the remainder of this book is to lay out a step-by-step programme for creating an integrated, synergistic motivation policy grounded in the belief that employees can simultaneously be high performers and achieve personal satisfaction. Given that one of the critical management skills discussed in this book involves proper diagnosis of performance problems, each section will be introduced using the appropriate diagnostic question shown in Table 1.

Table 1 Six elements of an integrative motivation programme

1. Establish moderately difficult goals that are understood and accepted.
   Ask: 'Do my people understand and accept what is required of them?'
2. Remove personal and organisational obstacles to performance.
   Ask: 'Do my people feel it is possible to achieve their objectives?'
3. Use rewards and discipline appropriately to prevent unacceptable behaviour and encourage exceptional performance.
   Ask: 'Do people accept the standards and that it is not acceptable to be a poor performer?'
4. Provide salient internal and external incentives.
   Ask: 'Do people feel the rewards used to encourage high performance are worth the effort?'
5. Distribute rewards equitably.
   Ask: 'Are work-related benefits distributed fairly?' or 'Are work-related rewards the correct way of rewarding individuals?'
6. Provide timely rewards and honest feedback on performance.
   Ask: 'Are the ways we reward effort useful and efficient?' 'Do people know where they stand in terms of current performance and long-term opportunities?'

The key assumptions underlying these six elements are:

1. Employees start out motivated. Therefore, a lack of motivation may be fostered by misunderstood or unrealistic expectations.
2. The role of management is to create a supportive, problem-solving work environment in which the necessary resources to perform a task are provided.
3. Rewards should encourage high personal performance which is consistent with management objectives.
4. Motivation works best when it is based on self-management.
5. Individuals should be treated fairly.
6. Individuals deserve timely, honest feedback on work performance.

Goal Setting

Managers should begin assessing the motivational climate of their work environment by asking, 'Do subordinates understand and accept my performance expectations?' The foundation of an effective motivation policy is proper goal-setting (Locke and Latham, 1984; Miner, 1984). The importance of goal-setting is so well recognised that it has been included in several formal management tools, such as 'management by objectives' (MBO). MBO is, however, regarded by many people as only partially providing an answer, ignoring the basic human needs for recognition (Stewart and Joines, TA Today, p72, 1987). Stewart and Joines argue that people need the recognition of others and that to only recognise failure is a profound mistake, leading to increased failure. People need to be recognised for themselves as what they do. Therefore, motivational goal-setting has three critical components: the goal-setting process itself, goal characteristics and feedback – for the persona and the task, good or bad.

A common theme of this book is that 'The way you do things is very often as important as what you do'.

This means that the process used to set goals must be understood and accepted if it is to be effective. Subordinates are more likely to own and accept the goals if they feel they were part of the generation process (Locke, Shaw, Saari and Latham, 1981). This is especially important if the work environment is unfavourable (Latham, Erez, Locke, 1988). For example, a goal might be inconsistent with accepted practice, require new skills, or exacerbate poor management–employee relations. The key to goal acceptance is an overall management attitude of understanding and support (Latham and Locke 1979). If this is not shown, then imposed goals or task-assignments will probably be viewed as unwelcome demands – subordinates will question the premises underlying the goal or assignment and will comply only with reluctance.

The ideal is sometimes difficult to achieve – a manager is sometimes 'given' goals by his or her own superiors without due consultation, and has to pass them on without sufficient understanding or discussion. However, if people believe management is committed to involving them wherever possible they will accept that there are times when things have to be done without question.

For example, a computer programming unit may not have any say about which application programs are assigned to the group or what priority is given to each incoming assignment. However, the manager can still involve unit members in deciding how much time to allocate to each assignment ('What is a realistic goal for completing this task?') or who should receive which job assignment ('Which type of programs would you find challenging?').

In 1974, Volvo, the Swedish motor car manufacturer, opened a new and radically different car assembly plant in Kalmar. It cost ten per cent more than a traditional factory to build, and the aim was to reduce the high labour turnover and absenteeism present in other Volvo plants.

Partially-built cars were transported on computer-controlled pods to work stations where groups of 15 to 20 workers (30 teams in the factory) performed a number of tasks, agreeing among themselves who would do what. The employees could rest in specially-designed rest areas whenever they wished, as long as certain agreed daily production targets were met. Workers enjoyed greater responsibility and jobs could be rotated.

Between 1977 and 1983 the production time per car fell by 40 per cent, the number of quality defects was reduced by 39 per cent and labour turnover was reduced from 25 per cent to five per cent. Volvo found that they needed fewer supervisors and that production flexibility was much higher. As a result a number of similar techniques were applied in their other plants.

Sources: *Financial Times,* 19 April 1985; *Management Today,* June 1988.

The Volvo experience was not without its critics and was not continued in its original form; the systems being largely taken over by what we will call 'Japanese management practices'.

The introduction of Japanese management practices has had a marked effect on British industry as the research of White and Trevor (1983) has shown:

> Japanese managers are well-regarded by their British subordinates because of their technical competence and their concern for high-quality work which was seen as reflecting upon workers and the reputation of the company. Being part of a competent and effective enterprise was what appeared to attract the British workers. So much so that the workers actually regarded with apprehension the eventual replacement of expatriate managers by the home-grown variety!
>
> Source: White M and Trevor M, *Under Japanese Management – the experience of British workers.* PSI Heineman. 1983.

But the Japanese have had to adapt their approach to take account of the culture gap. For instance, Toyota's UK's head of human resources, Brian Jackson admitted that British employees ask five times as many questions as their Japanese counterparts. When they opened their plant in Derby in December 1992 they laid down in great detail a standard way of undertaking any procedure. Employees were expected to stick to them but were also encouraged to recommend improvements. Everything is geared to continuous improvement – what the Japanese call 'Kaizen'.

At Toyota, employees, known as 'members', are divided into groups of about 25, headed by group leaders and sub-divided into teams of around four or five with team leaders. Each group normally meets about two or three times a day: first thing in the morning, mid-morning and mid-afternoon, each time for five or ten minutes, to discuss problems and ideas. Anyone can pull a cord or push a button to call over their team leaders if there is a problem and the line will stop if it cannot be resolved in seconds. Toyota don't just pay lip-service to the 'ideas' practice. For instance, in 1991 there were 40 suggestions from each Toyota employee in Japan and 90 per cent of them were adopted.

Shifting from process to content, research has shown that goal characteristics significantly affect the likelihood that the goal will be accomplished (Locke, Shaw, Saari and Latham, 1981). Effective goals are specific, consistent and appropriately challenging.

Woods and Whitehead (1993) discussed the concept of FRAME and goal setting. The acronym FRAME stands for Few, Realistic, Agreed, Measured and Explicit (see Table 2).

Specific goals reduce misunderstanding about what behaviours will be rewarded. Admonitions like 'be dependable', 'work hard', 'take initiative', or 'do your best' are too general and impossible to measure, and therefore of limited motivational value.

The manager has to be very clear in making the FRAME and during the process of translating the organisational goals to the individual goals. Handy's discretional goals need even more development of the organisational goals.

Only with a full understanding of what is happening can staff be motivated to enlarge their horizons towards the excellent performance.

American Express sees employee performance in three bands:

- Giving the customer what he or she wants and asks for – STANDARD
- Giving the customer what he or she wants but has not asked for – GOOD
- Giving the customer a service that he or she does not yet even know that he or she wanted – QUALITY WORLD-CLASS SERVICE

To provide an excellent or even a good service obviously needs a great deal of understanding of organisational objectives and capabilities.

Goals should also be consistent. An already hardworking general manager in a bank's regional office complains that she cannot increase both the number of reports she writes in a week and the amount of time she spends at branch offices, talking to employees and customers. Goals that are inconsistent, in the sense that they are logically impossible to accomplish simultaneously, or incompatible, in the sense that they both require so much effort that they can't be accomplished at the same time, create frustration and

Table 2 The concept of FRAME

	Explanation	*Example* – of a postal delivery worker (the information is NOT based on actual data but is intended for example only)
Few	Often the minutiae of a job is given. Goals should be confined to WHAT needs to be done, omit the HOW it is to be done and be as few in number as is reasonable. We are talking about STANDARD.	Deliver all the mail to the specified address or return it to the sorting office. Be available for work at 05.30 on regular days or notify the office in good time. Be honest.
Realistic	Miracles should not be called for; avoid such words as 'with no exceptions'. If the impossible is called for in any part of the goals it will become standard practice to allow ALL the goals to slip.	Obviously some mail will not be delivered or delivered to the wrong addresses perhaps because of mad dogs or snow. There must be an acceptable escape clause.
Agreed	Agreement means that the boss and the subordinate set up a dialogue – coaching and consultation as we discussed in the book – *Effective Communication*. The dialogue will weed out the impossible and establish commitment from the subordinate. Agreement is subject to constant feedback and review.	A new postal delivery worker will need to be coached to achieve the standard goals in the first place and every postperson is affected by external changes – population increase and decrease, new roads, etc.
Measured	The usual units are TIME and RESOURCES. This will be achieved at £'s cost in three months. For example, mile stone X, MUST be achieved, but it would also be good (excellent performance is judged by achieving) if milestone Y could be achieved.	The corporate objectives would be something like: 98% of all first class letters and packages delivered within 24 hours and 90% of all second class mail within 2 days within the agreed budget. The postperson's objectives must be inside the corporate objectives and within his of her span of responsibility.
Explicit	We have often found catch-all goals in job definitions – e.g., 'and such other activities and duties as the management may require'. If things are part of standard duties they should be laid down.	What we have said must be clear and put in such a way that new postpersons can inherit it successfully.

alienation. When subordinates complain that goals are incompatible or inconsistent, managers should be flexible enough to reconsider their expectations.

One of the most important characteristics of goals is the perceived level of difficulty (Latham and Locke, 1979; Locke, Shaw and Saari and Latham, 1981). Simply stated, hard goals are more motivating than easy goals. One explanation for this is called 'achievement motivation' (Atkinson and Raynor, 1974). A simple example of achievement motivation in action is the process of doing a crossword puzzle. The feeling of achievement in completing a full acrostic, as opposed to a simple tabloid word test is much greater. According to this perspective, workers size up new tasks in terms of 1) their chances for success and 2) the significance of the anticipated accomplishment.

Based only on perceived likelihood of success, one would predict that those who seek success would choose an easy task to perform, because the probability for success is the highest. However, most of us also take into account the significance of completing the task. To complete a goal that anyone can reach is not rewarding enough for highly-motivated individuals. They need to feel that the accomplishment represents a meaningful achievement. Given their desire for success and achievement, it is clear that these workers will be most motivated by challenging, but attainable goals.

The final component of an effective goal programme is **feedback** (Latham and Locke, 1979; Ivancevich & McMahon, 1982). Feedback provides opportunities for clarifying expectations, adjusting goal difficulty and gaining recognition. Therefore, it is important to provide benchmark opportunities for individuals to determine how they are doing. Reporting at milestones in the progress of projects is particularly critical when the time required to complete the total job or reach a goal is very long. Examples of milestone reporting would occur for an organisation writing a large computer program or raising a large sum of money for charity. In these cases feedback should be linked to accomplishing intermediate stages or completing specific components. The full use of the 'Small Wins' strategy is discussed in the book on *Effective Problem-Solving.*

The discussion of goal-setting has several important implications for managers.

- First, attention to the goal-setting process is important. Effective goals are both understood and accepted. Whether or not goals are imposed or self-generated, the process needs management support. One of the keys to self-motivation is self determination. Therefore, in a situation where a goal (what) is predetermined, management would do well to encourage participation regarding the means (who, how, when).
- Second, the characteristics of goals matter a great deal. The purposes of setting goals are to increase motivation and direct activity. These objectives are most likely to be accomplished when the goals are specific, consistent and difficult.
- Third, individuals should receive frequent feedback on their progress. A key ingredient of an effective motivational programme is sustainability, and a key to sustain ability is feedback.

Helping Subordinates' Achieve Their Objectives

One of the key ingredients of an effective goal-based programme is a supportive work environment. After goals have been set, the manager's focus should shift to **facilitating** a successful outcome and **monitoring** how individual goals fit into a whole. Therefore, the second diagnostic question is, 'Do subordinates feel it is possible to achieve this goal?'

Help from management must come in many forms, including making sure the worker has the required abilities for the job, providing the necessary training, securing needed resources, and encouraging co-operation and support from other work units. In other words, it is the manager's job to make the paths leading towards the targeted goals easier for the subordinate to travel.

An **enabling** role will vary considerably across individuals, organisational settings and tasks. If subordinates believe that strong management support is needed, but don't receive the help required then the manager will probably be regarded as being part of the employees' problem, rather than the source of solutions. By the same token, when management intervention is not needed or expected, managers who are constantly involved in the details of subordinates' job performance will be viewed as meddling and unwilling to trust. This view of management is incorporated in the views of House and Mitchell (1974).

The key question it addresses is 'How much help should a manager provide?' In response, the level of involvement should vary according to how much subordinates need to perform a specific task; how much they expect, in general; and how much support is available to them from other organisational sources.

The key task characteristics are structure and difficulty. A task that is highly structured (as reflected in the degree of built-in order and direction), and relatively easy to perform does not require extensive management direction. If managers offer too much advice, they will come across as controlling, bossy or nagging, since it is already clear to the subordinates what they should do. On the other hand, for an unstructured and difficult task, management's direction and strong involvement in problem-solving activities will be seen as constructive and satisfying.

The second factor that influences the appropriate degree of management involvement is the expectations of the subordinates. Three distinct characteristics influence expectations: desire for autonomy, experience and ability. Individuals who prize their autonomy and independence prefer managers with a highly participative, unobtrusive, leadership style because it gives them more latitude for controlling what they do. In contrast, people who prefer the assistance of others in making decisions, establishing priorities and solving problems welcome greater management involvement. However a self-motivated workforce may well *evolve* its goals, and the managers most difficult task is that of making sure that this evolution does not miss the overall goals of the organisation.

There is a direct connection between a worker's ability/experience level and the appropriate management style. Capable and experienced employees feel they need less assistance from their managers because they are adequately trained, know how to obtain the necessary resources and feel capable of handling political entanglements with their counterparts in other units. They appreciate managers who 'give them their head', but periodically check to see if further assistance is required. On the other hand, it is frustrating for relatively new employees, or those with marginal skills, to feel that their manager has neither the time nor interest to listen to basic questions.

The concept of the manager 'out of control' of the situation – the other side of the issue of subordinate autonomy, was brought to notice by the classical Hawthorne Studies (Roethlisberger and Dickson, 1939). In these studies a group of workers from the Hawthorne Works of the General Electric Company in the States were found to be able to organise their own work, in spite of major management intervention and very strong control mechanisms.

> The General Electric managers, later with support of academics, decided to see how work performance could be influenced by such external factors as heating and lighting levels. The job of assembling railway break equipment had been analysed in detail using Work Study techniques. For the experiment, they used two rooms of assembly workers doing virtually identical jobs. One room was to act as control and was left untouched during the tests, while the other was subjected to the series of planned experiments on working conditions. The results baffled the researchers at the time and are still the subject of argument and discussion. Put very briefly, whatever they did to the experimental group, including restoring all the conditions to their original settings, production improved.
>
> The initial conclusion was that the very act of recognising and showing an interest in workers was sufficient to improve productivity. The more contentious issue was – 'How was it possible for productivity to rise in an area where every movement in break assemble had literally been studied 'scientifically', noted and optimised?' Further observation and discussion with the workers themselves led to the conclusion that the work group itself had influenced the Work Study setting of rates to allow slack. Thus, the workers were able to adjust production and the bonus rates as they wished for 'local' reasons – 'Marge is getting married and needs the money'; 'It's coming up to Christmas and we ALL need the money'; 'If we are seen to work anywhere near capacity, they will only change the norms and reduce the bonus rates'.

When the work was originally done the paradigm used by the people who have used the Hawthorne case study was of workers somehow beating the system and 'surprisingly' being able to outsmart the managers. Much of this book is based on such a mind set. If we move on and change our mind set and develop a new paradigm – that of understanding that the workers at General Electric, as intelligent independent human beings, had asserted their rights to autonomy, and that there was great gain to be had in using their creativity and not attempting to restrict it in terms that were bound by class prejudice and elitism – we can begin to understand empowerment (the basis of the book *Effective Empowerment and Delegation*). Here we will look at the issue of empowerment, developing autonomy in individuals and groups, as a method of motivation.

James Gleick (1988) provides us with an elegant way of combining the concept of FRAME and motivation by empowerment. Willing workers given clear goals are the ONLY people who understand the minutiae of what is happening in their jobs. They, with the minimum of guidance, can make patterns of the inevitable local chaos of real working situations. Management beyond the minimum facilitation and monitoring reduce the creative dynamic or make useful order out of specific chaos.

Guest (1956) estimated that foremen engage in between 237 and 1,073 separate transactions a day. There is no possibility that these can be scheduled or planned – foreman are managing chaos and so are we all. The solution is to look at the processes in an organisation and to decide at what level WE are able to allow workers to be empowered – setting clear FRAMED goals and letting go.

One of the important lessons from this discussion is that managers must tailor their management style to specific conditions. Although managers should, in general, focus on facilitating task accomplishment, their level of direct involvement should be calibrated to the nature of the work and the availability of organisational support, as well as the ability and experience of the individuals. This conclusion underscores how important it is that managers understand the needs and expectations of their subordinates.

Richard Branson is one of the most inspirational leaders in British industry and he describes his philosophy as 'Small is Beautiful':

> In the early days we certainly could not have afforded a lavish corporate headquarters in central London. But now we don't have one as a matter of choice. It's not just that people prefer working in smaller units, but it helps to avoid some of the hazards of growth, and especially the tendency for managers to lose touch with the basics – and usually the customers and the staff.
>
> So when one of our companies gets beyond a certain size, we split it up into smaller units. Even though Virgin Records was, before we sold it to Thorn EMI, the sixth largest record company in the world, we managed through a series of semi-independent labels and subsidiaries in twenty countries.
>
> This 'keep it small' rule gives us the opportunity to pursue a policy of promoting from within the Group – a policy which clearly has a positive effect on morale. It means you can give more than the usual number of managers the challenge and excitement of running their own business. The kind of people I want running Virgin companies are those who would probably become millionaires if they weren't working for us. So if you can give them a stake in the company, they can become millionaires by working within Virgin.
>
> Source: *How To Get Ahead in Business*, Tom Cannon, Virgin Books, 1993.

Appropriate Use of Rewards and Discipline

Once clear goals have been established and the path to goal completion has been cleared by management, the next step in an effective motivational programme is to encourage goal accomplishment by linking performance to rewards and penalties. Therefore, the third diagnostic question is, 'Do subordinates feel that being a high performer is more rewarding than being a low or average performer?'

Our discussion of this important element of an effective motivational programme is based on two related principles:

1. In general, managers should link rewards to performance, rather than seniority.
2. Managers should be aware of the company objective, their own 'sub-objects' and manage their subordinates accordingly –

always noticing the person, rewarding and reinforcing productive behaviour and penalising non-productive behaviour in some way.

If an organisation is rewarding everybody to the same degree on some basis other than performance, then high performers are likely to feel they are receiving less than they deserve. Accepting that the most important individuals in any organisation are its high performers, systems to improve motivation in an organisation should be geared to keeping high performers happy. This observation has led some organisational consultants to use the performance ratings of individuals leaving an organisation as an index of the organisation's motivational climate. If the best people are leaving then a great deal is being said about the climate.

This motivation principle raises a voice of caution regarding the conventional practice in some organisations, of eliminating distinctions between workers. That is, some 'progressive' organisations have received considerable publicity for motivational programmes that include providing recreational facilities, library services, day care and attractive share option programmes for all employees. These organisations also work hard to reduce status distinctions by calling everyone 'associates' or 'partners', eliminating reserved parking places and instituting a company uniform. Although there are obvious motivational benefits to employees who feel they are receiving basically the same rewards regardless of seniority or level of authority, this motivational philosophy, when carried to an extreme or implemented indiscriminately, ends up demotivating high performers. In an era of egalitarianism, managers often overlook the vital link between performance and rewards, and as a consequence find it difficult to attract and retain strong performers.

In his book Maverick (Century, 1993) Ricardo Semler, CEO of the Brazilian company Semco, would not entirely subscribe to the views we have expressed. His company, making a range of white goods on licence, is certainly one of the most progressive and profitable organisations in the challenging financial climate of Brazil. Semler would claim to have a very highly-motivated workforce by any standard, but provides, as a matter of policy, *no fringe benefits* in the way of 'social services' for his employees. Commercial success is always the objective.

Semco does call its employees Partners, Co-ordinators and Associates and the organisation decided, in 1989, to allow Partners and Co-ordinators to set their own pay. This did not go far enough for Paulo Pereira, ex-personnel manager and now Co-ordinator of Semco, who went even further. He proposed the concept of 'risk salary' – 'Each one of you now has the correct salary, according to your own estimate of your worth. I propose to pay you a little less, but in return will give you the possibility of earning more.'

Semco is not alone in pioneering new motivational practices where commercial reality is coupled with empowerment and the concept of 'everybody wins'.

Zeneca, a company formed out of ICI to make speciality chemicals, working on the same concept as Semco, decided to remove all overtime payments. They set down a very simple principle:

Staff are only at work when they are needed. When they are at work they are effectively employed.

Zeneca has annualised the expected hours for which each employee is paid and added a significant and agreed number of hours for good measure. When there is no work, the employees stay at home; when there is work, they are called in and are expected to do any job for which they are able and competent and can be done by them safely.

The 'strange' by-product of the arrangement, which began in October 1993, is that the jobs that used to be done in overtime, have 'vanished'. An example is plant cleaning – the old practice was to do plant clean-ups during overtime and weekends; now the plant is kept clean and often no special cleaning shift is required. The same loss of a need for cleaning was noticed by British Gypsum operating the same principle.

Continental Can with 30 per cent of the total world production of cans, used a similar scheme and noted a similar 'remarkable' cure. The UK beer trade demanded a '15 per cent free beer offer' can which, obviously, is taller than the standard can. In production before the annualising of hours, the taller cans repeatedly fell over and had to be set up again by workers on overtime. Miraculously, with the new system, the cans did not fall over.

However do not expect cultural change to occur overnight, and certainly the transition to be simple – Scott-Morgan (1994) estimates that only 17 per cent of re-engineering of work processes are truly satisfactory. Raissa Rossiter (1995), agrees with eight per cent for a high level of success and 37 per cent for accepting changes as satisfactory, when she looked at several hundred companies implementing changes in working practice in the UK.

Technological constraints sometimes make it difficult to perfectly link rewards and individual performance. For example, people working on a motor car assembly line, or chemists working on a group research project, have little control over their personal productivity. In these situations, rewards linked to the performance of the work group will foster group cohesion and collaboration and partially satisfy the individual members' concerns about fairness. When it is not possible to assess the performance of a work group, a performance bonus should be considered. While the merits and technical details of various group and organisational reward systems are beyond the scope of this book, the point is that managers should link valued rewards and good performance at the lowest possible level of aggregation (Lawler, 1971; Greene, 1972). A word of warning should be expressed about general bonus payments – they may very soon come to be regarded as 'rights', and should they have to be withdrawn, may become a significant *demotivator*.

A second word of warning is concerned with team bonus arrangements. In principle the team is given a task and rewarded accordingly. The individuals within the team MAY perceive this as unfair.

> Bradford Management Centre, as many other business schools, use group assignments as part of the learning process. The written and oral presentations of these assignments went towards the ultimate grading of individual students. The process was abandoned by many of the staff because of the interminable claims of unfairness of the system:
>
> 'I carried that man, he did nothing towards the project except in the final presentation and he gets the same marks as me!'

Team bonus systems need to fit the culture but are very often a real problem when highly competitive individuals are concerned.

Effects of managers' responses.
An effective motivational programme goes beyond the design of the organisational reward system. Managers must also recognise that their daily interactions with subordinates can be important motivators. It is difficult for even highly sensitive and aware managers to fully understand the impact of their actions on the behaviour and attitudes of subordinates. Unfortunately, some managers don't even try to monitor these effects. The danger of this lack of awareness is that it may lead to managerial actions which actually reinforce undesirable behaviours in their subordinates. This has been called 'the folly of rewarding A while hoping for B' (Kerr, 1975). For example, a director of R&D with a low tolerance for conflict and uncertainty may unwittingly undermine the company's avowed objective of developing highly-creative products by punishing work groups that do not exhibit unity or a clear, consistent set of priorities. Further, while avowing the virtue of risk, the manager may punish failure; while stressing creativity, he or she may kill the spirit of the idea champion. These actions will encourage a work group to avoid challenging projects, suppress debate and develop task into routines.

The do's and don'ts for encouraging subordinates to assume more initiative (shown in Table 3), demonstrate the power of managers' actions in shaping behaviour. Actions and reactions that might appear insignificant to the boss often have strong reinforcing or extinguishing effects on subordinates. Hence the truism, 'Managers get what they reward, not what they want' and its companion, 'People do what is inspected, not what is expected'. Indeed, the reinforcing potential of managers' reactions to subordinates' behaviours is so strong it has been argued, that 'the best way to change an individual's behaviour in a work setting is to change his or her manager's behaviour' (Thompson, 1978). Given the considerable leverage managers have over their subordinates' motivation to reach optimal performance, it is important that they learn how to effectively use rewards and punishment to consistently produce positive intended results.

Table 3 Guidelines for fostering subordinate initiative

DO	*DON'T*
Ask, 'How are we going to do this? What can I contribute to this effort? How will we use this result?', thus implying your joint stake in the work and results.	Imply that the task is the employee's total responsibility, that they hang alone if they fail. Individual failure means organisation failure.
Use an interested, exploring manner, asking questions designed to bring out factual information.	Don't play the part of an interrogator, firing questions as rapidly as they can be answered. Also, avoid asking questions that require only 'yes' or 'no' replies.
Keep the analysis and evaluation as much in the employees' hands as possible by asking for their best judgement on various issues.	Don't react to their presentations on an emotional basis.
Do present facts about organisation needs, commitments, strategy, and so on, which permit them to improve and interest them in improving what they propose to do. Don't demand a change or improvement in a peremptory tone of voice or on what appears to be an arbitrary basis.	Don't redo their plans for them unless their repeated efforts show no improvement.
Ask them to investigate or analyse further if you feel that they have overlooked some points or over-emphasised others. Ask them to return with their plans after including these additional items.	Take their planning papers and cross out, change dates, or mark 'no good' next to certain activities.

Source: Kellogg, 1979, p 121

The process of linking rewards and punishment with behaviours in such a manner that the behaviours are more or less likely to persist is called 'operant conditioning' by psychologists (Skinner, 1953; Nord, 1975). This approach uses a wide variety of motivational strategies that involve the presentation or withdrawal of positive or negative reinforcers, or the use of no reinforcement whatsoever. Although there are important theoretical and experimental differences in these strategies, such as between negative reinforcement and punishment, for the purposes of our discussion we will simply focus on three types of management responses to employee behaviour: no response (ignoring), negative response (disciplining) and positive response (rewarding).

The trickiest strategy to transfer from the psychologist's laboratory to the manager's work environment is **no response**. Technically, what psychologists refer to as 'extinction' is defined as a behaviour followed by no response whatsoever. However, in most managerial situations, people develop expectations about what is likely to follow their actions, based upon their past experience, office stories etc. Consequently, what is intended as a non-response, or a neutral response, is generally interpreted as either a positive or negative response. For example, if a subordinate comes into your office complaining bitterly about a co-worker, and you attempt to discourage this type of behaviour by changing the subject or responding in a low, unresponsive monotone voice, the subordinate may view this as a form of rejection. If another subordinate sheepishly slips a report on your desk a week late, and you ignore his behaviour totally because you are busy with other business, he may be so relieved at not being reprimanded for his tardiness that he actually feels reinforced in failure.

These simple examples underscore an important point: any behaviour that is repeatedly exhibited in front of a boss is being rewarded, regardless of the boss' intention ('I don't want to encourage that type of behaviour, so I'm purposely ignoring it'). By definition, if a behaviour persists, it is being reinforced. If an employee is chronically late or continually submits sloppy work, the manager must ask where the reinforcement for this behaviour is coming from ('What am I or others doing to reinforce this behaviour?'). Consequently, while extinction plays an important role in the learning process if it is conducted in strictly controlled laboratory conditions, it is a less useful technique in organisational settings because the interpretation of a supposedly neutral response is impossible to control.

The **disciplining approach** basically involves responding

negatively to an employee's behaviour with the intention of discouraging future occurrences. For example, if an employee is consistently late, a supervisor may reprimand him with the hope that this action will decrease the employee's tardiness. Nagging subordinates for their failure to obey safety regulations is another example. Yet problems occur with the disciplining approach to shaping behaviour when it is used excessively or inappropriately.

The **rewarding approach** consists of linking desired behaviours with outcomes the employee will value. When a management trainee completes a report in a timely manner, the supervisor praises his promptness. If a senior executive takes the initiative to solve a thorny, time-consuming problem on her own, she could be given some extra time to enjoy a scenic location at the conclusion of a business trip. The value of positive reinforcement, according to Tom Peters and Bob Waterman (1982), is that it keeps the management–subordinate dialogue focused on 'nudging good things onto the agenda, rather than ripping bad things off the agenda'.

Disciplining and rewarding are both viable and useful techniques and each has its place in the effective manager's motivational repertoire. However, the techniques can produce quite different modifications of behaviour. Discipline should be used to begin the process of modifying unacceptable behaviours. However, once an individual's behaviour has reached an acceptable level, the process will cease to have a positive effect. It is very difficult to encourage employees to perform exceptional behaviours through nagging, threatening, or related forms of discipline. At a certain point subordinates fight against the criticism and don't improve their behaviour any further. Further improvement will only come through the positive reinforcement when employees have control over achieving what they want and, therefore, have the incentive to reach a level of exceptional performance. The same is true of rewarding behaviour. The positive reinforcement of desired behaviour has its downside in the avoidance of negative criticism – the manager needs to know when he or she should be firm.

The process of balance between discipline and rewards with unacceptable and acceptable behaviours, respectively, highlights two common misapplications of reinforcement principles.

First, it helps us better understand why top performers frequently get upset because they feel 'management is too soft on those people who are always messing things up'. Feeling it is good management practice to always be upbeat and optimistic, some managers try to ignore the seriousness of mistakes. They also try to temper the consequences by personally fixing errors, by encouraging high performers to be more tolerant and patient. Other managers feel so uncomfortable with confronting personal performance problems that they are willing to overlook all but the most flagrant mistakes.

Although there is a lot to be said for managers having a positive attitude and giving poor performers the benefit of the doubt, their failure to reprimand and redirect inappropriate behaviours leads to two undesirable outcomes: it poses a serious threat to the work unit's morale, and it does not improve the poor performer's behaviour.

Second, just as some managers find it unpleasant to issue reprimands for poor performance, other managers have difficulty praising exceptional performance. As a result, subordinates complain that 'nothing ever satisfies him'. This misapplication of the negative-response, behaviour-shaping strategy is just as dysfunctional as the indiscriminate use of praise. These managers mistakenly believe that the best way to motivate people is by always keeping expectations a little higher than their subordinates' best performance and then chiding them for their imperfection. In the process, they run the risk of burning out their staff or inadvertently encouraging lower performance (i.e., 'We'll get told off anyway, so why try so hard?'). Furthermore, the irony is that they create a competitive, self-defeating, situation in which the subordinates look forward to the boss making mistakes.

Unfortunately, many managers genuinely believe that this is the best way to manage – in all situations. They define their role as that of a sheepdog, circling the perimeter of the group, barking and nipping at the heels of those who begin to stray. Such managers establish a fairly broad range of acceptable behaviours and then limit their interactions with employees to restraining those who exceed the boundaries. This negative, desultory style of management creates a demoralising work environment and does not foster exceptional performance. Instead, workers are motivated to stay out of the boss's way and avoid doing anything unusual or untried. Innovation and involvement are extinguished, and mundane performance becomes not only acceptable but desirable.

> A laboratory managed by ex-scientists was a very happy place to work. People worked and lived together with very little to show between the levels of seniority. Positive reinforcement was the name of the game:
>
> *'That was a really good bit of work, perhaps a little late and over budget but . . . good all the same. A really good bit of work.'*
>
> Appraisals were also self congratulatory exercises until the company running the laboratory ran into trouble. Appraisals suddenly mattered and had to match the very patchy performance of the laboratory as a whole. Poor appraisal ratings meant that one's job was in jeopardy and the bad news had to be given by the managers who had NEVER given anything but praise before. At the end of the appraisal process several employees had taken legal action against the company and it was suspected that the efficiency of the laboratory took about three months to recover.

Having looked at the consequences of misapplying rewards and discipline, we will now turn our attention to the proper use of behaviour-shaping techniques.

Improving behaviours.

The mark of exceptional managers is fostering exceptional behaviour in their subordinates. They do this by making unacceptable behaviours acceptable and transforming the acceptable into exceptional. They are designed to avoid the harmful effects typically associated with the improper use of discipline discussed in the previous section (Hamner, 1974; Luthans & Kreitner, 1975; Maier, 1973) and they ensure the appropriate use of rewards (Latham, Cummings and Mitchell, 1981).

The nine steps for improving behaviours are shown in Table 4. These are organised into three broad initiatives: reprimand, redirect and reward. Steps 1-6 (reprimand and redirect) are used to extinguish unacceptable behaviours and replace them with acceptable ones. Steps 4-9 (redirect and reward) are used to transform acceptable behaviours into exceptional behaviours.

Table 4 Guidelines for improving behaviours

Reprimand

1. Identify the specific inappropriate behaviour. Give examples. Indicate that the action must stop.
2. Point out the impact of the problem on the performance of others, on the unit's mission, etc.
3. Ask questions about causes and explore remedies.

Redirect

4. Describe the behaviours or standards you expect. Make sure the individual understands and agrees that these are reasonable.
5. Ask if the individual will comply.
6. Be appropriately supportive. For example, praise other aspects of their work, identify personal and group benefits of compliance; make sure there are no work-related problems standing in the way of meeting your expectations.

Reward

7. Identify rewards that are important and of value to the individual.
8. Link the attainment of desirable outcomes with incremental, continuous improvement.
9. Reward (including using praise) all improvements in performance in a timely and honest manner.

As shown in Table 4, an important principle to keep in mind regarding the use of reprimands is that the discipline should immediately follow the faulty behaviour and focus only on the specific problem. This is not an appropriate time to dredge up old concerns or make general, unsubstantiated accusations. The focus of the discussion should be on eliminating a problem behaviour, not on making the subordinate feel bad. This will reduce the hostility typically engendered by being reprimanded. We will discuss this matter further in the book from the series, *Effective Communication*.

Secondly, an alternative behaviour should be suggested along with the discussion of what is seen to be wrong. It is important that persons being reprimanded understand how they can receive rewards in the future. This process of redirection reduces the despair that occurs when people feel they are likely to be punished no matter what they do.

If expected behaviours are not made clear, then individuals may stop the inapporpriate behaviour but feel lost, not knowing how to improve. Keep in mind that the ultimate goal of any negative feedback should be to transform inappropriate behaviours into appropriate behaviours (in contrast to simply punishing a person for causing a problem or making the boss look bad). The lingering negative affects of a reprimand will wear off quickly if the manager is soon able to reward desirable behaviours. This goal can be achieved only if workers know how they can receive positive outcomes.

Experienced managers know it is just as difficult to transform acceptable behaviours into exceptional ones. Helping a mediocre subordinate catch the vision of moving up to a higher level of desire and commitment can be very challenging. This process begins at Step 4 (redirect) by first clearly describing the goal or target behaviour. The goal of skilled managers is to avoid having to administer any negative responses and especially to avoid trial-and-error learning among new subordinates. This is done by clearly laying out their expectations and collaboratively establishing work objectives, following the guidelines discussed in an earlier section on goal-setting. In addition, it is a good idea to provide an experienced mentor, known for exceptional performance, as a sounding-board and role model.

Providing Salient Rewards

Having established a link between performance and outcomes (via rewards and discipline) as part of an integrative motivational programme, it is now important to focus on the salience of various outcomes. (To simplify the discussion we will focus only on rewards.) It stands to reason that performance will be enhanced only to the extent that the rewards attached to it are personally valued by the recipient. Our fourth diagnostic question, then is, 'Do subordinates feel the rewards used to encourage high performance are worth the effort?'

One of the biggest mistakes made in implementing a basically sound and well-intentioned reward system is that managers wrongly assume that they understand their subordinates' preferences. The manager's lament, 'What does Roger expect, anyway? I gave him a bonus, and he's still complaining to other members of the accounting department that I don't appreciate his superior performance', indicates an apparent miscalculation of what Roger really values.

The old accepted view on composition of portfolios of salient rewards is that they somehow change with job grade (LeDue, Jr, 1980 and others). Alisdair Galloway (1990) working with a large UK sample, found that designing an ideal portfolio of salient rewards was a difficulty for many managers. Predicting what rewards will be most salient to their subordinates requires individual knowledge and not approximations based on organisational status.

Table 5 Ranking of salient rewards for management, monthly and hourly-paid workers.

Salient reward	*Man'gt*		*Monthly paid staff*		*Hourly paid staff*	
	Average	*Standard deviation*	*Average*	*Standard deviation*	*Average*	*Standard deviation*
Wages/Salary	2.56	(2.84)	2.85	(4.87)	2.10	(3.96)
Job security	4.03	(4.42)	3.48	(7.17)	2.96	(5.42)
Job variety and interest	2.09	(3.28)	3.35	(5.84)	4.52	(5.45)
Freedom from supervision	5.78	(3.56)	5.73	(5.85)	6.69	(4.67)
Working conditions	6.34	(3.53)	5.37	(4.99)	3.67	(4.48)
Union org./activity	8.56	(2.00)	7.93	(5.23)	6.38	(6.06)
Promotion prospects	4.31	(3.46)	5.70	(7.94)	7.44	(5.99)
Control own work environment	4.34	(4.64)	5.10	(5.41)	6.10	(3.84)
Workmates	6.81	(3.19)	6.07	(5.43)	5.15	(3.98)

Source: Alisdair Galloway, 1990.

The very simple conclusion arising from Table 5 is that the average rankings are meaningless and the individual differences by far outweigh any collective considerations.

A flexible reward system helps managers avoid the second

common motivation mistake – projecting their preferences onto subordinates. Ineffective managers don't spend enough time with their workers to understand their personal needs and goals. Under these circumstances, it is quite natural for managers to assume that their subordinates share their views regarding the attractiveness of various job outcomes.

This judgement error is reflected in the case below:

> A fashion garment manufacturer lost its most skilled machinist – the person who was able to structure a new style into a form where it could be costed for production. The obvious choice for a replacement was an outstanding member of the production team who was widely respected by her shift mates. The woman was duly promoted and given a significant rise in salary. She was also given a little workroom of her own where she could concentrate on her work without being bothered by the noise and bustle of the shop floor.
>
> She handed in her notice in a matter of weeks – it was the noise and bustle that she liked – combined with being respected as the most skilled and experienced worker to turn to in time of trouble.

Unfortunately, this scenario is all too common. The practice of assuming similarity in preference across the workforce wouldn't be so detrimental if the population were relatively homogeneous. A 30-year longitudinal study of employee values at AT&T in America indicates that this is clearly not the case. For example, when new employees were asked during the 1950s what their goals were, 52 per cent focused on moving quickly up the corporate ladder into senior, well-paid jobs. In contrast, this goal was foremost in the minds of only 29 per cent of the respondents surveyed in the 1970s. The second sample expressed less loyalty to the job and placed more emphasis on personal fulfilment. In the words of the survey's co-ordinator, Doug Bray, 'It's a whole new idea permeating society. People feel that no job is worth killing themselves for or devoting their lives to' (Colby, 1985).

Effective managers avoid problems by having frequent, personal and supportive discussions with their subordinates – a subject covered in detail in the book of this series, *Effective Communication*. These exhanges should focus on career opportunities, life goals and personal priorities. Another technique used by managers is discussing with subordinates recent significant changes in the careers of common acquaintances. Subordinates' responses to changing circumstances affecting others (pay, personal time, travel requirements etc.) often provide useful insights into their personal preferences.

Maslow's 'Hierarchy of Needs' suggests that they are a priority as well as a dynamic element in human needs. At the most basic level, individuals begin with physiological needs – the basic life-sustaining needs. Once these are satisfied they can consider personal security, and when these two needs are satisfied they proceed to the first of the social needs – belonging and relating to others. Once this simple belonging need is satisfied we move to the higher need for esteem, and finally to the need for personal growth – self-actualising, as Maslow called it. As individuals fulfil a specific need, they shift their focus to the next highest hierarchical level. Satisfied needs become dormant until a dramatic shift in circumstances rekindles them. For example, a middle-level executive who is fired during a hostile take-over may suddenly find her interest in personal growth is overwhelmed by a pressing need for security. Other major events that may shift an individual's need priorities include a birth or death in the family, marriage or divorce, job transfer or job obsolescence, promotion or demotion. Effective managers are sensitive to shifts in their subordinates' needs and accommodate those shifts by implementing flexible organisational reward systems.

Internal job characteristics.

All of the outcomes shown in Table 5, except for 'interesting work', are called external motivators because they are controlled by someone other than the worker – typically by the immediate supervisor. The supervisor can show appreciation for a job well done, offer job security, show personal loyalty to employees and provide good working conditions. It is a slightly different story for 'interesting work'. Although managers control the components of a job, they have no direct control over whether a specific subordinate finds a job interesting. In other words, the outcomes associated with an interesting job come from internal motivators – factors inherent in the job itself, not from any particular actions of the manager.

Effective motivators understand that the person-job interface has a strong impact on how an employee performs the job. No matter how many externally controlled rewards managers use, if their subordinates find their jobs to be uninteresting and unfulfilling, performance will suffer. Attention to internal motivators is particularly critical in situations where managers have relatively little control over the organisational incentive system. In these cases it is often possible to compensate for lack of control over external factors by fine-tuning the person-job fit.

Job design is the process of matching job characteristics and workers' skills and interests. One popular job-design model proposes that particular job dimensions cause workers to experience specific psychological reactions, called 'states'. In turn, these psychological reactions produce specific personal and work outcomes. Figure 2 shows the relationship between the core job dimensions, the psychological states they produce, and the resulting personal and work outcomes (Hackman and Oldham, 1980). According to this model, intrinsically satisfying tasks are high on skill variety, task identity, task significance, autonomy and feedback.

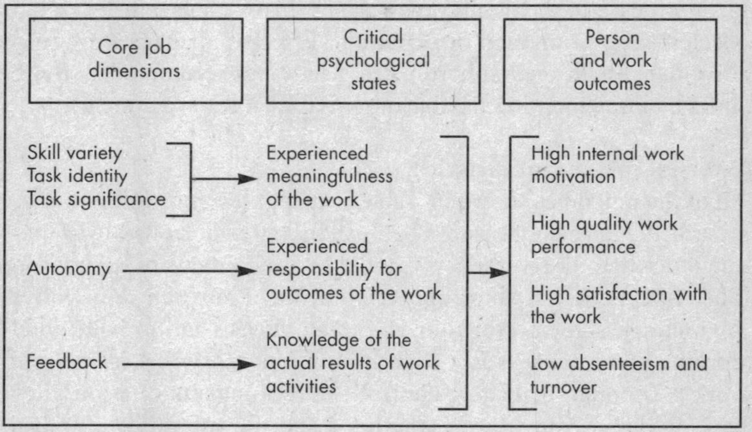

FIGURE 2 Designing highly motivating jobs

Source: adapted from Hackman and Oldham, 1980.

The more variety in the skills a person can use in performing the work, the more the person perceives the task as being meaningful or worthwhile. Similarly, the more an individual can perform a complete job from beginning to end (task identity), and the more the work has a direct effect on the work or lives of other people (task significance), the more the employee will view the job as meaningful. On the other hand, when the work requires few skills, only part of a task is performed, and there seems to be little effect on others' jobs, experienced meaningfulness is low. The effect of such dull repetitive work on job performance will again depend on the individual.

> A legend has it that a major chocolate manufacturer gives IQ tests to all its job applicants for shop floor work. If the candidates passed the minimum standard – THEY DO NOT GET THE JOB. The history was that the brighter applicants worked harder, quicker and better than their duller counterparts for a few weeks and that then their work rates began to fall. Left in the job, they became the trouble makers. It was noted also that several workers resisted any attempt to develop their jobs: 'It's a lousy job anyway – I do it for the money and I think about what I'm going to do when the whistle blows. I don't want to have to think.'

Autonomy can in itself enrich work and improve performance. As we have said before, the nearer a manager can achieve the role of monitor and facilitator the better. Autonomy can be increased by instituting flexible work schedules, decentralising decision making, or removing selected formalised controls such as the ringing of a bell to indicate the beginning and end of the work day.

Finally, the more feedback individuals receive about how well their jobs are being performed, the more knowledge of results they have. This permits workers to understand the benefits of the jobs they perform. This can be enhanced by increasing employees' direct contact with clients or by giving them feedback on how their jobs fit in and contribute to the overall operation of the organisation.

By enhancing the core job dimensions and increasing critical psychological stages, job fulfilment is increased. Job fulfilment (high internal work motivation) is associated with other outcomes valued by management. These include high-quality work performance, high satisfaction with the job, low absenteeism and high turnover. In other words, employees who have well-designed jobs enjoy doing them because they are intrinsically satisfying.

The 'Employment in Britain' study, which surveyed 5,000 people in the UK in 1992 pointed to relatively inexpensive means employers can use to make jobs more attractive and engender greater loyalty without altering pay. The report found that money and job security were important but that real influence over the way work was done and over the organisation as a whole was highly valued by employees – and conversely was a source of frustration when absent.

John Stevens, a director of the Institute of Personnel Management in the UK, said 'At one time we tended to treat many people in the workforce as semi-detached from the organisation. Competitive pressure, decentralisation and awareness of the need to develop skills, have merged what people want out of work and what employers want out of people'.

This view is echoed by Hakan Aström, COE of Sweden's Kabi pharmaceutical group. He says, 'Management is about getting the commitment and involvement of those around you. You get the best out of people if they have been involved in the decision-making process and understand why a decision has been taken'.

Michael Hammer and James Champy in their book *Reengineering the Corporation* (1993) developed five principles of job design:

1. **Combine tasks.** A combination of tasks is by definition a more challenging and complex work assignment. It requires workers to use a wider variety of skills, which makes the work seem more challenging and meaningful. For example, telephone directories at the former Indiana Bell Telephone company used to be compiled in 21 steps along an assembly line. Through job redesign, each worker was given the responsibility for compiling an entire directory.
2. **Form identifiable work units** so that task identity and task significance may be increased. Clerical work in a large insurance firm was handled by 80 employees organised by functional

task (e.g., opening letters, entering information into the computer, sending out statements). Work was assigned based on current workload by a supervisor over each functional area. To create higher levels of task identity and task significance, the firm reorganised the clerical staff into eight self-contained groups. Each group handled all business associated with specific clients.

3. **Face the customer** (Greenberg and Ornstein, 1984). A client relationship involves an on-going personal relationship between an employee (the producer) and the customer, internal or external. We need to recognise the value of this relationship, both for the motivation of the work teams and the organisation. At its highest level, for example, at GKN each customer group – Toyota, GM, BMW/Rover – has a specific GKN team attached. At much lower levels, Cottage Holidays, a holiday home lease business, identifies a particular telephone sales representative with each customer and this person acts as the name contact point.
4. **Grant more authority for making job-related decisions to those actually doing the jobs.** As supervisors delegate more authority and responsibility, their subordinates' perceived autonomy, accountability and task identity increase. Historically, workers on motor car assembly lines have had little decision-making authority. However, in conjunction with increased emphasis on quality, many plants now allow workers to adjust their equipment, reject faulty materials, and even shut down the line if a major problem is evident.
5. **Open feedback channels.** Workers need to know how well or how poorly they are performing their jobs if any kind of improvement is expected. It is imperative that they receive timely and consistent feedback which allows them to make appropriate adjustments in their behaviour so they can receive desired extrinsic and intrinsic rewards. The traditional approach to quality assurance is to 'inspect it in'. A separate quality assurance group is assigned to check the quality of the production team. The emerging trend is to give producers responsibility for checking their own work. If it doesn't meet

quality standards, they immediately fix the defect. Following this procedure, workers receive immediate feedback on their performance.

Although this management tool, like others, involves trade-offs, the record of job redesign interventions is impressive. Depending on the approach taken, firms typically report a substantial increase in productivity, work quality and worker satisfaction (reflected in lower rates of absenteeism). For example, General Electric realised a 50 per cent increase in product quality as a result of their job-redesign programme, while the absenteeism rate among data-processing operators at Traveller's Insurance decreased by 24 per cent (Kopelman, 1985).

In conclusion, this section on external and internal rewards contains two important lessons for managers:

- Make sure there are enough reward options available for subordinates so they can personally select salient outcomes. The motivational potential of an effective goal-setting process and a supportive, obstacle-removing management style is dissipated if employees feel that high performance will not lead to personally attractive outcomes.
- Recognise that both external and internal outcomes are necessary ingredients of effective motivational programmes. In particular, ignoring internal outcomes can significantly undermine a manager's efforts to motivate. Most people want interesting and challenging work activities. Good wages and job security will do little to overcome the negative effects of individuals' feeling that their abilities are being under-utilised.

Equitable Distribution of Rewards

Once the appropriate rewards have been determined for each employee, the manager must then consider how to distribute the rewards (Greenberg, 1982). This brings us to concerns about equity. Any positive benefits of salient rewards will be negated if workers feel they are not receiving their fair share. (As in the previous section, we will focus only on rewards. However, the same basic principles also apply to the equitable use of discipline.)

Equity refers to workers' perceptions of the fairness of rewards. Evaluations of equity are based on a social comparison process in which workers individually compare what they are getting out of the work relationship (outcomes) with what they are putting into the work relationship (inputs). Outcomes include such items as pay, fringe benefits, increased responsibility and prestige, while inputs may include hours worked and work quality, as well as education and experience. The ratio of outcomes to inputs is then compared to corresponding ratios of other individuals judged to be an appropriate comparison group. The outcome of this comparison is the basis for beliefs about fairness.

If workers experience feelings of inequity, they will behaviourally or cognitively adjust their own, or fellow workers', inputs and/or outputs. In some cases, this may lead to a decrease in motivation and performance. For example, if employees believe that they are being underpaid, there are a number of options available to them. Cognitively, they may rationalise that they really are not working as hard as they thought they were; thus they reduce the perceived value of their own inputs. Alternatively, they might convince themselves that co-workers are actually working harder than they thought they were. Behaviourally, workers can request a pay rise (increase their outcomes), or they can decrease their inputs by leaving a few minutes early each day, decreasing their effort, deciding not to complete an optional training programme, or finding excuses not to accept difficult jobs.

Other more 'mechanical' inequities may also be exposed. For example, the hourly rate of a worker may not be keeping up with recent skill upgrades or increased job responsibilities. The act of identifying and correcting legitimate inequities generates enormous commitment and loyalty. For example, a manager in the computer industry felt he had been unfairly passed over for promotion by a rival. Utilising the company's open-door policy, he took his case to a higher level in the firm. After a thorough investigation, the decision was reversed and the rival reprimanded. The individual's response was, 'After they went to bat for me, I could never leave the company.'

The important thing to keep in mind about equity and fairness is that we are dealing with perceptions. Consequently, whether they are accurate or distorted, legitimate or ill-founded, until proven otherwise they are both accurate and legitimate in the mind of the perceiver. A basic principle of social psychology is 'That which is perceived as being real is real in its consequences.' Therefore, effective managers should constantly perform 'reality checks' on their subordinates' perceptions of equity, using questions such as: 'If you were asked to match yourself with one or two others in this department, who would you pick as most similar?', 'What criteria for promotions, pay rises and so on do you feel management should be placing more/less emphasis on?', 'Relative to others similar to you in this organisation, do you feel your job assignments, promotions and so on are appropriate?', 'Why do you think Anne was recently promoted over John?'

Providing Timely Rewards and Accurate Feedback

Minimising the time lag between behaviours and feedback, and providing accurate feedback are our final topics in the integrated approach to motivation. The sixth diagnostic question is: 'Are we getting the most out of our rewards by administering them on a timely basis, as part of the feedback process?'

Up to this point we have emphasised that employees need to understand and accept performance standards; they should feel that management is working hard to help them reach their performance goals; they should feel that the internal and external rewards available are personally attractive; they should believe that rewards and reprimands are being distributed fairly; and they should feel that these outcomes are being administered primarily on the basis of performance.

All these elements are necessary for an effective motivational programme, but they are not sufficient. Rewards, even highly-valued ones, lose their motivating potential unless they are dispersed at the correct time. It is the timing of the reinforcement that lets the employee know which behaviours are being encouraged. Giving a reward at the wrong time can inadvertently increase an undesirable behaviour. For example, giving a long-overdue, fully warranted rise to a subordinate during an interview in which she or he is complaining about the unfairness of the reward system, may reinforce complaining rather than good work performance. Moreover, failure to give a reward when a desired behaviour occurs will make it even more difficult to increase that behaviour in the future. If the owners of a new business have delayed the implementation of a promise to grant share options for the core start-up team as compensation for their low wages and 70- to 80-hour work-weeks, the willingness to sustain this pace on only promises and dreams may begin to wane.

The importance of timing becomes obvious when one considers that all the research findings supporting the value of operant conditioning as a motivational system assume that outcomes immediately follow behaviours. Imagine how little we would know about behaviour-shaping processes if, in the experiments with birds and rats described in psychology textbooks, the food pellets were dropped into the cage several minutes after the desired behaviour occurred.

Unfortunately, although timing is a critical aspect of reinforcement, it is frequently ignored in everyday management practice. The formal administrative apparatus of many organisations often delays for months the feedback on the consequences of employee performance. It is customary practice to restrict in-depth discussions of job performance to formally designated appraisal interviews, which generally only take place once every six or twelve months. This delay between performance and feedback dilutes the effectiveness of any rewards or discipline dispensed as a result of the evaluation process.

In contrast, effective managers understand the importance of immediate, spontaneous rewards. They use the formal performance evaluation process to discuss long-term trends in performance, solve problems inhibiting performance, and set performance goals. But they don't expect these infrequent, general discussions to provide much motivation. For this they rely on brief, frequent, highly salient performance feedback. For example, at least once a week they seek some opportunity to praise desirable work habits among their subordinates.

Peters and Waterman stress the importance of immediacy with story of the Hewlett Packard Banana award (1982).

> At Hewlett Packard, a technical advance was desperately needed for survival in the company's early days. Late one evening, a scientist rushed into the president's office with a working prototype. Dumbfounded at the elegance of the solution and bewildered as to how to reward it, the president bent forward in his chair, rummaged through most of the drawers in his desk, found something, leaned over the desk to the scientist, and said, 'Here!' In his hand was a banana, the only reward he could immediately put his hands on. From that point on, the small gold banana pin has been the highest accolade for scientific achievement at Hewlett Packard.

Effective rewards are spontaneous rewards. Rewards that become rituals, especially those linked to formal performance appraisal systems, lose their immediacy. A prize awarded to almost anyone soon loses its appeal.

There is a second critical aspect – the consistency of giving rewards. Administering a reward every time a behaviour occurs is called continuous reinforcement. Administering rewards on an intermittent basis (the same reward is always used but is not given every time it is warranted) is referred to as partial, or intermittent reinforcement. Neither approach is clearly superior; they both have drawbacks. Continuous reinforcement represents the fastest way to establish new behaviour. For example, if a boss consistently praises a subordinate for writing reports using the manager's preferred format, the subordinate will readily adopt that style in order to receive more and more rewards. However, if the boss suddenly takes an extended leave of absence, the learned behaviour may cease because the reinforcement pattern is broken. In contrast, while partial reinforcement results in very slow learning, it is very resistant to extinction. The persistence associated with gambling behaviour illustrates the addictive nature of a partial reinforcement schedule. Not knowing when the next pay-off may come preserves the myth that the jackpot is only one more try away.

This information about reinforcement timing derives from experimental research and has important implications for effective management.

- First, it is important to realise that continuous reinforcement systems are very rare in organisations unless they are mechanically built into the job, as in the case of the piece-rate pay plan. Seldom are individuals rewarded every time they make a good presentation or effectively handle a customer's complaint. When we recognise that most non-assembly-line work in an organisation is typically governed by a partial reinforcement schedule, we gain new insights into some of the more frustrating aspects of a manager's role. For example, it helps explain why new employees seem to take forever to catch on to how the boss wants things done. It also suggests why it is so difficult to extinguish outdated behaviours, particularly in older employees.

- Second, given how difficult it is for one manager to consistently reinforce the desired behaviours in a new employee (or an employee who is going through the reprimand, redirect, reward cycle), it is generally a good idea to use a team effort. By sharing your developmental objectives with other individuals who interact with the target employee, you increase the likelihood of the desired behaviours being reinforced during the critical early stages of improvement. For example, if a division head is trying to encourage a new member of her staff to become more assertive, she might encourage other staff members to respond positively to the newcomer's halting efforts in meetings or private conversations.

Content and intent of the feedback.

Before concluding this discussion of feedback, it is important to add a brief note about the message itself. The second part of the sixth diagnostic question related to feedback is: 'Do subordinates know where they stand in terms of current performance and long-term opportunities?'

In addition to the timing of feedback, the content of the feedback and motivation guiding the feedback process can have a powerful impact on the target individual's willingness and ability to improve. If the content is inaccurate, improvement is frustratingly difficult. If the message is masked in subterfuge and obscured by mixed messages, the credibility of the entire motivational system is undermined.

The book from this series – *Effective Communication*, discusses the premise that it is much more difficult to deliver bad news than good news. That book contains a number of guidelines and principles for providing negative feedback in a non-threatening, constructive manner. Our purpose now is not to review that material, but only to stress the importance of being honest and open with subordinates regarding their current performance and future opportunities. The time-worn excuses, 'We don't want to run the risk of discouraging marginal performers' and 'We shouldn't tell people their future promotion opportunities are in jeopardy because upper management doesn't like their style', generally constitute efforts to cloak managers' feelings of discomfort under the guise of doing what's best for the subordinate.

Reluctance to share unflattering or unhopeful feedback is usually an admission by managers that they are unwilling to spend sufficient time with the individuals receiving negative feedback to help them thoroughly understand it, put it in perspective, consider options and explore possible remedies. It is simply easier to pass on an employee with a poor performance record or unrealistic expectations to the next supervisor than it is to confront the problem directly, provide honest and constructive feedback, and help the individual respond appropriately. That is why many feel that supportive communication of negative performance information is the most difficult to master, and therefore the most highly prized management skill.

Summary

Our discussion of enhancing work performance has focused on specific analytical and behavioural management skills. We first introduced the fundamental distinction between ability and motivation. Several diagnostic questions for determining whether inadequate performance was due to insufficient ability were discussed. Also, a five-step process for handling ability problems (refurbish, retrain, redeploy, reassign and release) was outlined. Motivation was introduced by stressing the need for placing equal emphasis on concerns for satisfaction and performance. The remainder of the book focused on the second skill by presenting the six elements of an integrative approach to motivation.

The summary model shown in Figure 3 encompasses our discussions of ability and motivation. This flowchart depiction of the factors influencing performance and satisfaction underscores the interdependence between the various components. Skilled managers incorporate all elements of this model into their motivational efforts rather than concentrating only on a favourite subset. There are no shortcuts to effective management. All elements of the motivation process must be included in a total, integrated programme for improving performance and satisfaction.

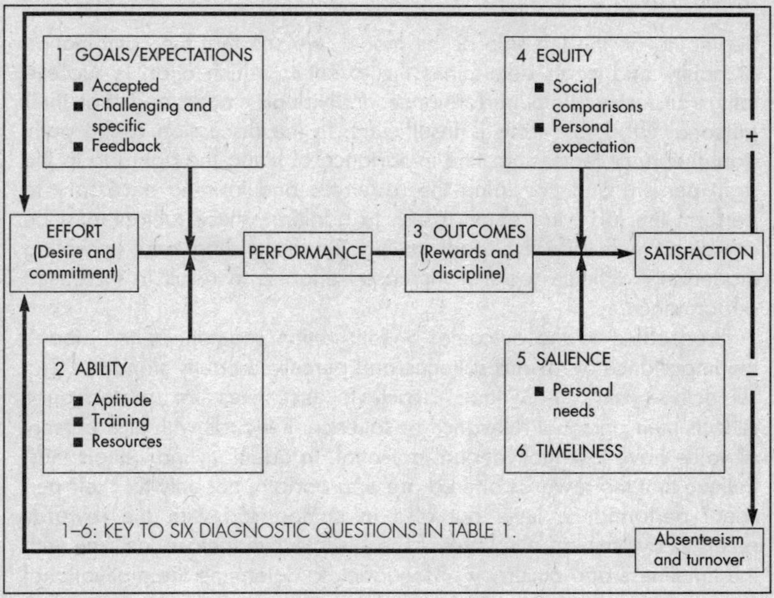

FIGURE 3 Model of motivation enhancement

The flowchart begins with effort. Remember that motivation is manifested as work effort, and that effort consists of desire and commitment. Motivated employees have the desire to initiate a task and the commitment to do their best. Whether their motivation is sustained over time depends on the remaining elements of the model, which are organised into two major segments:

1. The effort > performance link
2. The outcomes > satisfaction link

These two crucial links in the motivational process can best be summarised as rhetorical questions pondered by individuals asked to work harder, change their work routine, or strive for a higher level of quality.

First, 'If I put in more effort, am I likely to be able to perform up to expectations?'
Second, 'Am I likely to find being a high performer personally rewarding?'

Beginning on the left side of the model, we see that the combination of ability and goals determines the extent to which effort is successfully transformed into performance. Individuals understand that their personal effort, by itself, is insufficient. In the discussion of the path-goal theory of leadership, the importance of fitting the right job to the right person, and providing the resources and training necessary to perform the job were emphasised. In addition, these factors must be combined with effective goal setting (understanding and accepting moderately difficult goals) if increased effort is to result in increased performance.

Proceeding to the outcomes > satisfaction segment of the model, the importance of reward salience and perceived equity stand out. The subjective value individuals attach to incentives for performance reflects their personal relevance or salience. Rewards with little personal value have low motivational potential. In addition, individuals must believe that the rewards offered are appropriate, not only for their personal performance level but also in comparison with the rewards received by 'similar' employees. These subjective factors combine with the timeliness and accuracy of feedback to determine the motivational potential of rewards.

Based upon the perceptions of their outcomes, workers will experience varying degrees of satisfaction or dissatisfaction. Satisfaction creates a positive feedback loop, increasing the individual's motivation, as manifested by increased effort. Dissatisfaction, on the other hand, results in decreased effort and, therefore, lower performance and rewards. If uncorrected, this pattern may ultimately result in absenteeism or high staff turnover.

Behavioural Guidelines

This discussion has been organised around key diagnostic models and questions. These serve as the basis for enhancing the skills of 1) properly diagnosing performance problems, 2) initiating actions to enhance individuals' abilities and 3) strengthening the motivational aspects of the work environment.

The process for properly diagnosing the causes of poor work performance is summarised in the form of six diagnostic questions, shown in Table 1, page 18. (A 'decision tree' version of these questions is included in the Skill Practice section, page 69.) The behavioural guideline governing this process is:

1. Investigate work performance problems fully.
   - Separate ability from motivation problems
   - Agree on a programme for improving performance
   - Release a poor performer only as a last resort

The key guidelines for enhancing ability and creating a highly-motivating work environment are:

2. Define an acceptable level of overall performance or specific behavioural objectives clearly.
   - Make sure the individual understands what is necessary to satisfy your expectations
   - If possible, formulate goals and expectations collaboratively
   - Make goals as difficult as possible

3. Help remove all obstacles to reaching the objective.
   - Make sure the individual has adequate technical resources, personnel and political support
   - If a lack of ability appears to be hindering performance, use the refurbish, retrain, redeploy, reassign or release series of remedies

4. Make rewards and discipline contingent on high performance or drawing nearer to the behavioural objective.
   - Carefully examine the behavioural consequences of your 'non-responses' (Ignoring a behaviour is rarely interpreted as a neutral response)
   - Consistently discipline individuals whose effort is below your expectations and their capabilities

5. When discipline is required, treat it as a learning experience for the individual.
   - Specifically identify the problem and explain how it should be corrected
   - Use the reprimand and redirect guidelines in Table 4, page 39
6. Transform acceptable into exceptional behaviours.
   - Reward each level of improvement
   - Use the redirect and reward guidelines in Table 4, page 39
7. Use reinforcing rewards that appeal to the individual.
   - Allow flexibility in individual selection of rewards
   - Provide both appealing external rewards as well as satisfying and rewarding work (intrinsic satisfaction)
   - To maintain salience, do not overuse rewards
8. Check subordinates' perceptions regarding the equity of reward allocations periodically.
   - Correct wrong perceptions that serve as the basis for equity comparisons
9. Minimise the time lag between behaviours and feedback on performance, including the administration of rewards or reprimands. (Spontaneous feedback shapes behaviour best.)
   - Provide honest and accurate assessments of current performance and long-range opportunities

Skill Analysis

Case Involving Motivation Problems

Electro Logic

The Organisation

Electro Logic (EL) is a small R&D firm located in the Midlands (UK), near to a major university. Its primary mission is to perform basic research on, and the development of, a new technology called 'Very Fast, Very Accurate' (VFVA). Founded four years ago by David Morton, an electrical engineering professor who invented the technology, EL is primarily funded by government contracts, although it plans to market VFVA technology and devices to commercial organisations within the year.

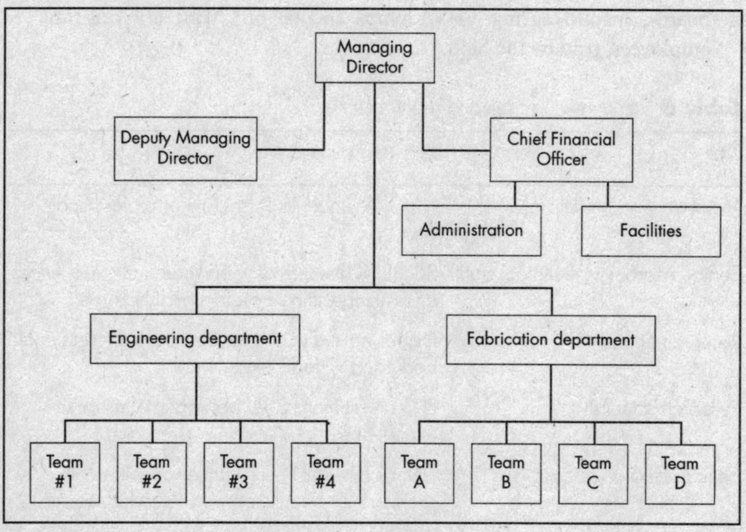

FIGURE 4 Electro Logic organisation chart

The government is very interested in VFVA, as it will enhance radar technology, robotics, and a number of other important defence applications. EL recently received the largest small-business contract ever awarded by the government to research and develop this or any other technology. Phase I of the contract has just been completed and the government has agreed to Phase II contracting as well.

The organisational chart of EL is shown in Figure 4 (page 59). Current membership is 75 of which about 90 per cent are in engineering. Heads of staff are supposedly appointed according to their knowledge of VFVA technology and their ability to manage people. In practice, the managing director of EL hand-picks these people based on what some might call arbitrary guidelines – most of the staff leaders are David Morton's graduate students. There is no pre-determined time frame for advancement up the hierarchy. Salary increases are, however, directly related to performance appraisal evaluations.

Working directly with the engineers are the technicians. These people generally have a university degree. They are trained on the job, although some have gone through a local college's programme on microtechnology fabrication. The technicians perform the mundane tasks of the engineering department: running tests, building circuit boards, manufacturing VFVA chips and so on. Most are full-time employees, paid by the hour.

Table 6 Engineering titles and requirements

Title	*Required qualification*
Member of technical staff	HNC, Member or Associate of professional body
Senior member of technical staff	BSc (ENG) with two years industrial experience and membership of professional body
Research engineers	PhD or equivalent – membership of professional body and 7 years experience
Research scientist	PhD or 1st Hons BSc, appropriate research experience
Senior research scientist	DSc or relevant PhD Member or Fellow or professional body. Appropriate industrial and research experience

The administrative staff is composed of the staff head (a woman with an MBA from a major university), accountants, personnel director, graphic artists, purchasing agent, project controller, technical writers/editors and secretaries. Most of the people on the administrative staff are women. All are hourly-paid employees except the staff head, the personnel director and the project controller. The graphic artists and technical writers/editors are part-time employees.

External contractors are used for maintenance and are controlled by the Facilities Department. EL is housed in three different buildings, and the primary responsibility of the facilities staff is to ensure that the facilities of each building are in good working order. Additionally, the facilities staff are often called upon to remodel parts of the buildings as staff numbers continue to grow.

EL anticipates a major recruiting campaign. In particular, it is looking for more technicians and engineers. Before this recruiting campaign, however, the managing director of EL hired an outside consultant to assess employee needs as well as the morale and overall effectiveness of the firm. The consultant has been observing EL for about three weeks and has written up some notes of her impressions and observations of the company.

Consultant's Notes from Observations of Electro Logic

Facilities: EL is housed in three different buildings. Two are converted houses and one is an old school building. Senior managers and engineers are in the school; others are scattered between the houses.

Meetings: Weekly staff meetings in the main building are held to discuss objectives and to formulate and review milestone charts.

Social interaction: A core group of employees interact frequently on a social basis, e.g., sports teams, parties. The administration staff celebrate birthdays at work. The managing director occasionally attends.

Work allocation: Engineers request various tasks from the support staff – technicians and administrative unit personnel. There is obviously some discretion used by the staff in assigning priorities to the work requests, based on rapport and desirability of the work.

Turnover: The highest turnover is among administration personnel and technicians. Exit interviews with engineers indicate that they leave because of the company's crisis-management style, better opportunities for career advancement and security in larger organisations, and overall frustration with EL's 'pecking order'. Engineers with the most responsibility and authority tend to leave.

Salaris and benefits: In general, wages at EL are marginal by national and local standards. A small group of scientists and engineers do make substantial salaries and have a very attractive benefits package, including share options. Salaries and benefits for new engineers tend to be linked to the perceived level of their expertise.

Offices and facilities: Only EL's managing director, deputy managing director, and chief financial officer have their own offices. Engineers are grouped together in 'pods' by project assignment. There is very little privacy in these work areas and the noise from the shared printer is distracting.

The head of administration shares a pod with the personnel director, facilities head and the project controller. One to three secretaries per building are located in or near the reception areas.

The large building has an employee lounge with three vending machines. There is also a coffee and tea area. The smaller buildings have only a cold drinks machine in the reception area.

Consultant's Interviews with Employees

After making these observations, the consultant requested interviews with a cross-section of the staff in order to compile a company survey. Below are excerpts from these interviews.

Pat Donaldson, senior member of technical staff

Consultant: What is it about Electro Logic that gives you the most satisfaction?

Pat: I really enjoy the work. I've always liked to do research and working on VFVA is an incredible opportunity. Just getting to work with David Morton (EL's managing director and VFVA's inventor) again is exciting. I was his student about six years ago. He really likes to work closely with his people – perhaps sometimes too closely. There have been times when I could have done with a little less supervision.

Consultant: What is the least satisfying aspect of your work?

Pat: Probably the fact that I'm never quite sure that we'll be funded next month, given the defence budget problems and the tentativeness of our research. I've got a family to consider and this place isn't the most financially stable. Perhaps it'll change once we get more into commercial production.

Consultant: You've offered some general positives and negatives about Electro Logic. Can you be more specific about day-to-day dealings? What's good and bad about working here on a daily basis?

Pat: You're sure this isn't going to get back to anyone? OK? Well, in general I'm not satisfied with the fact that too often we end up changing horses midstream. In the past seven months, three of my engineers and four of my technicians have been pulled off my project onto projects with deadlines which were nearer than mine. Now I'm faced with a deadline and I'm supposed to be getting more staff – but I'll have to spend so much time briefing them that it might make more sense for me to just finish the project myself. On the other hand, David keeps telling me that we have to be concerned with EL's overall goals, not just our individual concerns – you know, we have to be 'team players' and 'good members of the family'. It's hard to remember that though, when deadlines are bearing down and you know your neck is on the line, team player or not. But if you go along with this philosophy and don't complain, the higher-ups treat you well. Still, it seems to me there's got to be a better way to manage these projects.

Consultant: What are the positive aspects of your daily work?

Pat: The people are great to work with. I tend to be a social person and I really like playing in the darts team. I've got some good friends here which helps get my work orders filled quickly, if you know what I mean.

Bob Keegan, member of technical staff

Consultant: You said earlier that David Morton was your advisor for your Masters degree. So you've known him a long time.

Bob: Yes, that's right. I've known Professor Morton – David – for about eight years. I had him for a few undergraduate classes, then, of course, he was my advisor for my Masters programme, and now I've worked at EL for two years.

Consultant: It seems as if you enjoy working with David.

Bob: Oh, yes. But I really don't get to work directly with him anymore. I'll see him at meetings but that's about it.

Consultant: So he's not your immediate supervisor?

Bob: No, but for the amount of time I spend with my supervisor, David might as well be. My boss and I meet perhaps once every three weeks for about an hour to see if all is well. And that's it. The rest of the time, I'm on my own. I used to talk to David when I had questions, but he's so busy these days that it's hard to see him – you need to make an appointment a few days in advance.

Consultant: Do you think your supervisor treats all his staff this way?

Bob: To be honest, I have heard some complaints. In fact, about six months ago, the situation was so bad some other people and I had a meeting with him. He promised that he would be more available to us, and he was – for about a month. Then we got involved in a new proposal and he made himself scarce again. So nothing's really changed. We're finalising the proposal now and it's important that I see him to ask him questions. The last few drafts I've submitted to him, he's returned, rewritten in his own way and with no explanation of the changes. Sometimes I think he treats me like somebody who doesn't know anything, as if I had no training whatsoever. I realise his neck is on the line with this project, but it seems that he uses being busy to avoid talking to me.

Chris Chan, research scientist

Consultant: What kind of characteristics should a person have if he/she wants to work as a research scientist at Electro Logic?

Chris: Well, certainly technical knowledge is important –when I've interviewed recent graduates I insist they have got a good degree. But for experienced research scientists, technical knowledge shows up in their publication records, mostly. So I'll read their papers. I also think a research scientist has to be highly self-motivated, not look to others for praise. Particularly here. If you want someone to tell you you've done a good job, you'll be waiting a long time. It's not clear to me that research scientists really get the support we need from the rest of the staff here. Work orders are often lost or put off for one reason or another. Senior members seem to get more technicians than scientists do and they certainly get more attention from David. The rumour is that these people also get higher rises than the scientists; allegedly, this is to keep pay at an equitable rate – you know, they're supposedly more valuable to the company. Of course, everybody knows that most of the senior members are David's old graduate students, and so he takes care of them really well. One of the things that really galls me is that I need to keep up my publication record to maintain my career options, but publishing is frowned on here because it takes time away from your work. I've even been told that my work can't be published because of proprietary rights or that the defence department considers the information classified. However, if somebody important is working with me and needs the publication, then it's full steam ahead.

Consultant: You sound pretty disgruntled with your work.

Chris: It's not my work so much. I'm really very happy doing this work – it's cutting-edge, after all. The problem is that I'm never quite sure where the work is going. I do my part of a project, and unless I go out of my way to talk to other people I never find out the final results of the total project. That's just something you learn to live with around here – being part of a system that's not particularly open.

Margaret Conroy, assistant to the head of administration

Consultant: You've only been here a short time, is that correct?

Margaret: That's right – just a little over a year.

Consultant: Why did you take the job?

Margaret: Well, I was in my last term at university and was looking for a job, like most students. My fiancée at the time – now he's my husband – was already working for EL and found out that there was an opening. So I applied.

Consultant: Were you taking business studies at university?

Margaret: Oh, no. I was taking history.

Consultant: Do you like your job?

Margaret: It has a lot to offer. I get paid well for what I'm doing. And I'm learning a lot. I just wish the company would let me take some courses in administration, like accounting. The auditors ask some pretty tough questions. David says we should hire that expertise, but I'd still be responsible for supervising the people.

Consultant: Is there any particular aspect about your job that you really find satisfying?

Margaret: Well, let me see. I like the fact that I can do lots of different tasks so that things don't get so boring. I would hate to have to do the same thing, day in and day out. A lot of the time, I go to the library to do research on different things, and that's nice because it gets me out of the office.

Consultant: What don't you like about your job?

Margaret: Well, I often get the feeling that administration isn't taken seriously. You know, the engineers could get along without us quite nicely or so they seem to think. The whole structure of the departments shows that we're the catch-all department – if you don't fit anywhere else, they put you in here. Perhaps some of that is because our department is primarily women – in fact, I've been told that 95 per cent of all the female employees are in administration. Sometimes it's hard to work with the engineers because they treat you like you don't know anything – and they always want things to be done their way. Clearly, the engineers get the money and consideration and yet, well, we do contribute quite a lot to the whole team, as David would say. But words of praise just aren't as impressive as actions. We get our birthday parties, but that still seems to be a little patronising. We rarely get to see what's going on in the research area. I've asked a number of engineers some specific questions, and they just look at me with a blank stare and give me some really simplified answer. It seems to me if you want to build a team, like the boss says, you can't treat administration like a bad relation.

Gareth Roberts, technician

Consultant: I gather you've just been through your biannual performance appraisal. How did it go?

Gareth: Like I expected. No surprises.

Consultant: Do you find these appraisals useful?

Gareth: Yes. I get to find out what he thinks of my work.

Consultant: Is that all?

Gareth: Well, I suppose it's a nice opportunity to understand what my supervisor wants. Sometimes he's not so clear during the rest of the year. I suppose he's been given specific goals from higher-ups before he talks with me, so he's clear and then I'm clear.

Consultant: Do you like what you're doing?

Gareth: Of course. The best part is that I'm not at the main building and so I don't have to put up with the 'important' people, you know? I've heard from other technicians that those people can be a real bore – trying to be nice, but really just being a nuisance. I mean, how can you get your work done when the managing director's looking over your shoulder all the time. On the other hand, if the MD knows your name, I suppose that's a good thing when it comes to rises and promotions. But my boss sticks up for his technicians – we get a fair deal from him.

Consultant: Do you think you'll be able to get ahead at Electro Logic?

Gareth: Get ahead? You mean become an engineer? No, and I really don't want to do that. Everyone here keeps pushing me to move up. I'm afraid to tell people how I really feel for fear they'll decide I don't fit into this high-tech environment. I like doing what I do and if the rises keep coming, I'll keep liking it. One of my daughters is starting college next year and I need the money to help her out. I get a lot of overtime, particularly when contract deadlines are near. I suppose the rush towards the end of contracts gives some people big headaches, but for me I don't mind. The work is pretty slow otherwise, and so at least I'm working all the time. But my family wishes my schedule was more predictable.

Consultant: Do you think you'll continue working for Electro Logic?

Gareth: I'm not sure I want to answer that. Let's just say that my ratings on the performance appraisal were good and I expect to see an improvement in my pay. I'll stay for that.

Chelsey Montgomery, technician

Consultant: In general, what are your feelings about the work you do for EL?

Chelsey: Well, I feel my work is quite good, but I also feel that I perform rather boring, tedious tasks. From what my supervisor says, the kinds of things I do are what electrical engineering students do in their last year in college. I gather their final project is to make a circuit board, and that's what I do, day in and day out.

Consultant: What is it that you would like to do?

Chelsey: Well, it would be nice to be able to offer some input into some of the designs of these boards. I know I don't have a PhD or anything, but I do have lots of experience. But because I'm a technician the engineers don't really feel I've got much to offer – even though I build the boards and can tell from the design which one will do what, the designer wants to do it. I also would like to supervise other technicians in my department. Some kind of advancement would be nice. As it is, lots of technicians ask me how to do things and of course I help, but then they get the credit. Around here, you have to have a piece of paper that says you're educated before they let you officially help other people.

Discussion Questions

1. Using the Behavioural Guidelines (page 57) and Figure 3 (page 55) as diagnostic aids, what are the strengths and weaknesses of Electro Logic from a motivational perspective?
2. What are the high-priority action items you would include in a consulting report to David Morton, managing director of Electro Logic? Focus on specific actions that he could initiate that would better use the abilities of the staff and foster a more motivating work environment.

Skill Practice

Exercises for Diagnosing Work Performance Problems

Background

Proper diagnosis is a critical aspect of effective motivation management. Often managers become frustrated because they don't understand the causes of observed performance problems. They might experiment with various 'cures', but the inefficiency of this trial-and-error process often simply increases their frustration level. In addition, the accompanying misunderstanding adds extra strain to the manager–subordinate relationship. This generally makes the performance problem even more pronounced, which prompts the manager to resort to more drastic responses, and a vicious, downward spiral ensues.

The performance diagnosis model in Figure 5 (next page) offers a systematic way for managers and subordinates to collaboratively pinpoint the cause(s) of dissatisfaction and performance problems. It assumes that employees will work hard and be good performers if the work environment encourages these actions. Consequently, rather than jumping to conclusions about poor performance stemming from deficiencies in personality traits or a bad attitude, this diagnostic process helps managers focus their attention on improving the selection, job design, performance evaluation and reward allocation systems. In this manner, the specific steps necessary to accomplish work goals and management's expectations are examined to pinpoint why the worker's performance is falling short.

The manager and low-performing subordinate should follow the logical discovery process in the model, step by step. They should begin by examining the current perceptions of performance, as well as the understanding of performance

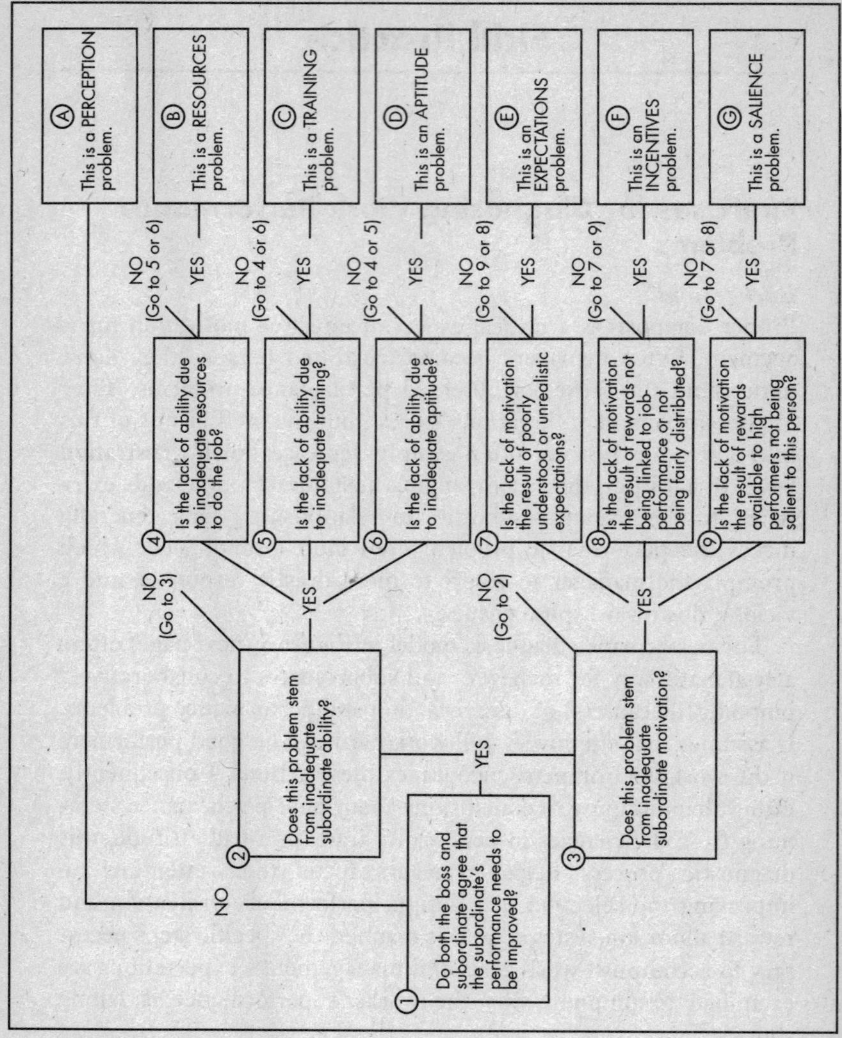

FIGURE 5 Performance diagnosis model

expectations, and then proceed through the model until the performance problems have been identified. The model focuses on seven of these problems.

A. Perception problem: 'Do you agree your performance is below expectations?' A perception problem suggests that the manager and subordinate have different views of the subordinate's current performance level. Unless this disagreement is resolved, it is futile to continue the diagnostic process. The entire problem-solving process is based on the premise that both parties recognise the existence of a problem and are interested in solving it. If agreement does not exist, the manager should focus on resolving the discrepancy in perceptions, including clarifying current expectations (Problem E).

B. Resources problem: 'Do you have the resources necessary to do the job well?' (Ability has three components, and these should be explored in the order shown in the model. This order reduces a subordinate's defensive reactions.) Poor performance may stem from a lack of resource support. Resources include material and personnel support as well as co-operation from interdependent work groups.

C. Training problem: 'Is a lack of training interfering with your job performance?' Individuals may be asked to perform tasks that exceed their current skill or knowledge level. Typically this problem can be overcome through additional training or education.

D. Aptitude problem: 'Do you feel this is the right job/blend of work assignments for you?' This is the most difficult of the three ability problems to resolve because it is the most basic. If the refurbish (providing additional resources) and retraining solutions have been explored without success, then more drastic measures may be required. These include redeploying the person's current job requirements, reassigning him to another position, or, finally, releasing him from the organisation.

E. Expectations problem: 'What are your performance expectations for this position? What do you think my expectations are?' This problem results from poor communication regarding job goals or job requirements. In some cases, the stated goals may be different from the desired goals. In other words, the employee is working toward one goal while the supervisor desires another. This often occurs when subordinates are not sufficiently involved in the goal – or standard-setting process. When this results in unrealistic, imposed expectations, motivation suffers.

F. Incentive problem: 'Do you believe rewards are linked to your performance in this position?' Either the individual does not believe that performance makes a difference or insufficient performance feedback and reinforcement have been given. The manager should also ask, 'Do you feel rewards are being distributed equitably?' This provides an opportunity to discuss subordinates' criteria for judging fairness. Often, unrealistic standards are being used.

G. Salience problem: 'Are the performance incentives attractive to you?' Salience refers to the importance an individual attaches to available rewards. Often, the incentives offered to encourage high performance simply aren't highly valued by a particular individual. The salience problem points out the need for managers to be creative in generating a broad range of rewards, and flexible in allowing subordinates to choose among rewards.

Assignment

Option 1: Read the case, 'George's performance problems', and privately use the diagnostic model (Figure 5, page 70) to pinpoint plausible performance problems. Next, in small groups discuss your individual assessments and list the specific questions you should ask George to accurately identify, from his point of view, the obstacles to his high performance. Finally, brainstorm ideas for plausible solutions. Be prepared to represent your group in role-playing a problem-solving interview with George.

Option 2: Administer the Work Performance Assessment survey (found in the Pre-assessment section, page 5) to several employees. Using the associated Scoring Key at the back of the book (page 84), categorise the obstacles to high performance and satisfaction reported by the respondents. Then get together in small groups, each one assuming the role of a management task force charged with the responsibility of analysing these employee survey data. Discuss the patterns in the data as well as possible remedies for the problems, using the Behavioural Guidelines and motivational models in this book as guides. Be prepared to make a report on your analysis, and recommendations for specific changes.

George's Performance Problems

George joined your architectural firm two years ago as a draughtsman. He is 35 and has been a draftsman since leaving technical college. He is married and has four children. He has worked for four architectural firms in 12 years.

George came with mediocre recommendations from his previous employer, but you employed him because you needed help desperately. Your firm's workload has been extremely high due to a local construction boom. The result is that a lot of the practices that contribute to a supportive, well-managed work environment have tended to be overlooked. For instance, you can't remember the last time you conducted a formal performance review or did any career counselling. Furthermore, the tradition of closing the office early on Friday for a social hour was dropped long ago. Unfortunately, the tension in the office runs pretty high some days due to unbearable time pressures and the lack of adequate staff. Evening and weekend work have become the norm rather than the exception.

Overall, you have been pleasantly surprised by George's performance. Until recently he worked hard and consistently produced high-quality work. He frequently volunteered for special projects, made lots of suggestions for improving the work environment, and has demonstrated an in-depth practical knowledge of architecture and the construction business. However, during the past few months, he has definitely eased off. He doesn't seem as excited about his work, and several times you have found him daydreaming at his desk. In addition, he has got into several heated arguments with architects about the specifications and proper design procedures for recent projects.

After one of these disagreements, you overheard George complaining to his office partner, 'No one around here respects my opinion. I'm just a lowly draughtsman. I know as much as these trendy architects, but because I don't have the degree, they ignore my views, and I'm stuck doing the donkey work. Adding insult to injury, my wife has had to get a job to help support our family. I must be the lowest-paid person in this firm.'

In response to a question from a co-worker about why he didn't pursue a university degree in architecture, Joe responded, 'Do you have any idea how hard it is to put bread on the table, pay the mortgage, work overtime, be a reasonably good father and husband, plus go to evening classes? Come on, be realistic!'

Exercise in Reshaping Unacceptable Behaviours

Background

One of the most challenging aspects of management is transforming inappropriate behaviours into appropriate behaviours. Managers commonly take insufficient action to transform negative actions into positive ones. Some of these insufficient responses include: assuming that ignoring the problem will make it go away; praising positive aspects of an individual's performance in the hope that it will encourage him or her to re-channel unproductive energies; discussing the problem in vague, general terms in a group meeting in the hope that the unproductive person will 'take a hint' and change; getting upset with the individual and demanding that he or she 'sort themselves out'.

Assignment

Assume the role of Andrew Tate in the following case. After reading the case (do not read the role instructions for Ruth), be prepared to role-play your discussion with Ruth in a small group. Obviously, one member of this group should play Ruth while the others assume the role of observers. Prior to the role-play, the observers should familiarise themselves with the Observer's Feedback Form in the Scoring Key (page 85). They should then proceed to complete this form during the role-play so that the group can discuss the results after the role-play has ended.

Ruth's Tardiness

Andrew Tate, manager

Ruth has been a member of your staff for only three months. You don't know much about her except that she is a single parent who has recently entered the work force after a difficult divorce. She is often ten to 20 minutes late for work in the morning. You are the manager of a very hectic customer relations office for a utility company. The phones start ringing promptly at eight o'clock. When she is late for work, you have to answer her phone, and this interrupts your schedule. This morning you are particularly annoyed. She is 25 minutes late and the phones are ringing furiously. Because you have been forced to answer them, it will be difficult for you to complete an important assignment by the noon deadline. You are getting more annoyed by the minute.

While you are in the middle of a particularly unpleasant phone conversation with an irate customer, you look out of your window and see Ruth bounding up the steps to the building. You think to yourself, 'This is ridiculous, I've got to put a stop to her lateness. Maybe I should just threaten to sack her unless she sorts herself out.' Upon further reflection, you realise that would be impractical, especially during this period of retrenchment after the new wage demand was turned down. Given the rumours about a possible freeze on recruitment, you know it may be difficult to refill any vacancies.

Also, Ruth is actually a pretty good worker when she is there. She is conscientious and has a real 'knack' with irate callers. Unfortunately, it has taken her much longer than expected to learn the computer program for retrieving information on customer accounts. She frequently has to put callers on hold while she asks for help. These interruptions have tended to increase an already tense relationship with the rest of the office staff. She has had some difficulty fitting in socially; the others are much younger and have worked together for several years. Ruth is the first new appointment in a long time, so the others aren't used to breaking someone in. Three of your staff have complained to you about Ruth's constant interruptions. They feel their productivity is going down as a result. She also seems to expect them to drop whatever they are doing every time she has a question. They had expected their workload to be lighter when a new person was hired, but now they are having second thoughts. (In the past you have had enough time to train new recruits, but your boss has had you tied up on a major project for almost a year.)

Ruth enters the office obviously flustered and dishevelled. She has 'I'm sorry' written all over her face. You motion for her to pick up the phone and then scribble a note on a notepad while you complete your call: 'See me in my office at 12.00 sharp!' It's time you got to the bottom of Ruth's disruptive influence on an otherwise smooth-flowing operation.

Ruth Call, staff member

What a morning! Your baby-sitter's Dad died during the night, and she called you from the railway station at 6.30 to say she would be away for three or four days. You tried three usually available backups before you finally found someone who could look after Katie, your three-year-old. Then Sarah was really difficult over her breakfast. It's a miracle that Brian, your oldest, was able to pull himself out of bed after getting only five hours sleep. On top of soccer and drama, he's now joined the chess team and they had their first tournament last night. Why did it have to fall on the night before his final in physics? This morning you wished you had his knack for juggling so many activities. By the time you got the children sorted out, you were already ten minutes behind time. Then there was this incredible accident on the motorway that slowed traffic to a crawl.

As you finally pull off the slip road, you notice you're almost twenty minutes late for work. 'My kingdom for a car phone!' you groan. 'Although by now I probably couldn't get an open line into the office, anyway.' As you desperately look for a parking space, you begin to panic. 'How am I going to explain this to Mr Tate? He'll be furious. I'm sure he's upset about my chronic lateness. On top of that, he's obviously disappointed with my lack of computer skills, and I'm sure the others complain about having to train a newcomer.' You're sure that one of the reasons you got the job was that you had completed a computer course at the local community college. Unfortunately, it didn't really prepare you for the incredibly complex computer program you use at work – it seems to defy every convention of logic.

'What am I going to tell him about my being late for work so often?' Unfortunately, there isn't an easy answer. 'Maybe it will get better as the children and I get used to this new routine. It's just very difficult to get the children to the bus stop and the baby-sitter, commute twenty minutes, and arrive precisely at 8.00 o'clock. I wonder if he would allow me to come in at 8.30 and only take a half-hour lunch? Staying late wouldn't work because they close down the computers at 5.00, unless there was some paperwork I could do for half an hour.'

And then what about the problems with the computer and the other women? 'Sooner or later he's going to get on to me about those things. Is it my fault I don't think like a computer? Some people might be able to sit down and figure this program out in a couple of hours, but not me. So is that my fault or should someone be giving me more training? I wish the others weren't so cliquish and unwilling to help me out. I wonder why that's the case? It's like they're afraid I'll become as good as they are if they share their experience with me. I wish Mr Tate had more time to help me learn the ropes, but he seems to always be in meetings.'

'Well, I'm probably going to catch it this morning. I've never been this late. Maybe I'll be back home full-time sooner than I expected.'

Skill Application

Application Activities For Motivating Others

Suggested Further Assignments

1. Identify a situation in which you have some responsibility for another person whose performance is significantly below your expectation. Using the Work Performance Assessment Survey included in the Pre-assessment section (page 5), collect information on the individual's perceptions of the situation. Using the diagnostic model (decision tree) in that section, specifically identify the perceived performance problems. Compare these results with your own views of the situation. Conduct an interview with the individual and discuss the results, highlighting areas of disagreement. Based on this discussion, formulate a plan of action that both parties accept. If inadequate ability is a problem, follow the re-furbish, retrain, redeploy, reassign and release remedial steps. If insufficient effort is a problem, use the steps for reprimanding, redirecting and rewarding discussed in this book. Implement this plan for a period of time and then report on the results.
2. Focus on some aspect of your own work in which you feel performance is below your (or others') expectations. Using the Work Performance Assessment Survey, identify the specific obstacles to improved performance. Then formulate a plan for overcoming these obstacles, including getting commitments from others. Discuss your plan with individuals affected by it and arrive at a set of actions all parties accept. Implement the plan for a period of time and report on your results. How successful were you in making the changes? Did your performance improve as expected? Based on this experience, identify other aspects of your work that you could improve in a similar fashion.
3. Identify four or five situations in which you are typically provoked to exhibit punishing behaviour. These might involve friends, family members or work associates. Examine these situations and identify one where punishment (discipline) is simply not working. Using

the guidelines for reprimanding, redirecting and rewarding, design a specific plan for shaping the other person's behaviours so you can begin rewarding positive actions. Report on your results. Based on this experience, consider how you might be able to use this strategy in other similar situations.

4. Using the six-step model for creating a motivating work environment (Table 1, page 18), design a specific plan for managing a new relationship (e.g., a new subordinate) or a new phase in an old relationship (e.g., friend, family member or subordinate about to begin work on a new project). Write down specific directions for yourself for implementing each of the six steps. Discuss your plan with this individual and ask for suggestions for improvement. Make sure your perceptions of the key aspects of the plan are consistent with his or hers. Implement your plan for a period of time and then report on the consequences. Based on this experience, identify changes that would be appropriate in similar settings.

Application Plan and Evaluation

The intent of this exercise is to help you apply your skills in a real-life, out-of-class setting. Now that you have become familiar with the behavioural guidelines that form the basis of effective skill performance, you will improve the most by trying out those guidelines in an everyday context. The trouble is, unlike a classroom activity in which feedback is immediate and others can assist you with their evaluations, this skill application activity is one you must accomplish and evaluate on your own. There are two parts to this activity. Part 1 helps prepare you to apply the skill. Part 2 helps you evaluate and improve on your experience. Be sure to actually write down answers to each item. Don't short-circuit the process by skipping steps.

Part 1 – Planning

1. Write down the two or three aspects of this skill that are most important to you. These may be areas of weakness, areas you most want to improve, or areas that are most salient to a problem you currently face. Identify the specific aspects of this skill that you want to apply.

2. Now identify the setting or the situation in which you will apply this skill. Establish a plan for performance by actually writing down the situation. Who else will be involved? When will you do it? Where will it be done?
3. Identify the specific behaviours you will engage in to apply this skill. Operationalise your skill performance.
4. What are the indicators of successful performance? How will you know you have succeeded in being effective? What will indicate that you have performed competently?

Part 2 – Evaluation

5. After you have completed your implementation, record the results. What happened? How successful were you? What was the effect on others?
6. How can you improve? What modifications can you make next time? What will you do differently in a similar situation in the future?
7. Looking back on your whole skill practice and application experience, what have you learned? What has been surprising? In what ways might this experience help you in the long term?

Scoring Key

Diagnosing Poor Performance and Enhancing Motivation

To find your score for each skill area, add your rating scores together for the relevant questions.

Skill area	*Question no.*	*Assessment pre-*	*post-*
Diagnosing performance problems	1,11	_____	_____
Establishing expectations and setting goals	2,12	_____	_____
Facilitating performance (enhancing ability)	3,13,20	_____	_____
Linking performance to rewards and discipline	5,6,14,15	_____	_____
Using salient internal and external incentives	7,8,16,17	_____	_____
Distributing rewards equitably	9,18	_____	_____
Provided timely and straightforward performance feedback	4,10,19	_____	_____
TOTAL SCORE		_____	_____

To assess how well you scored on this instrument, compare your scores to three comparison standards:

- Compare your scores against the maximum possible (120).
- Compare your scores with the scores of other students in your class.
- Compare your scores to a norm group consisting of 500 business school students. In comparison to the norm group, if you scored:

  101 or above, you are in the top quartile;
  94 to 101, you are in the second quartile;
  85 to 93, you are in the third quartile;
  84 or below, you are in the bottom quartile.

Work Performance Assessment

Instructions

Step 1: Enter your score from each line below, as follows:

Regular scoring: Enter the number for your response on the survey.
Reverse scoring: Subtract the number of your response from 6 and enter the result.

Items	*Score*	*Items*	*Score*
1. Reverse	_____	8. Regular	_____
2. Reverse	_____	9. Regular	_____
3. Reverse	_____	10. Regular	_____
4. Reverse	_____	11. Regular	_____
5. Reverse	_____	12. Regular	_____
6. Reverse	_____	13. Regular	_____
7. Reverse	_____	14. Regular	_____

Step 2: Combine your scores according to the type of performance problem. Problems with scores higher than 7 are obstacles to high performance. Total scores over 50 suggest significant, broad-based motivational deficiencies.

Type of Performance Problem	*Scores on items*			*Total of two items*
Perception	1: _____	+ 8: _____	=	_____
Training	2: _____	+ 9: _____	=	_____
Aptitude	3: _____	+ 10: _____	=	_____
Resources	4: _____	+ 11: _____	=	_____
Expectations	5: _____	+ 12: _____	=	_____
Incentives	6: _____	+ 13: _____	=	_____
Reward salience	7: _____	+ 14: _____	=	_____
TOTAL SCORE				_____

Observer's Feedback Form

Reshaping Unacceptable Behaviours

Ruth's Tardiness

ACTION	**RATING** (1=low, 5=high)
Reprimand	
1. Identified the specific inappropriate behaviour. Gave examples. Indicated that the action must stop.	______
2. Pointed out the impact of the problem on the performance of others, the unit's mission, etc.	______
3. Asked questions about causes and explored remedies.	______
Redirection	
4. Described the behaviours or standards expected. Made sure the individual understood and agreed that these are reasonable.	______
5. Asked if the individual would comply.	______
6. Was appropriately supportive. For example, praised other aspects of the person's work, identified personal and group benefits of compliance, and made sure there were no legitimate obstacles in the way of meeting stated expectations.	______
Reward	
7. Identified rewards that were salient to the individual.	______
8. Linked the attainment of desirable outcomes with incremental, continuous improvement.	______
9. Rewarded (included using praise) all improvements in performance in a timely and honest manner.	______

Comments:

Glossary

Ability	The product of aptitude improved by training and opportunity. The skills to perform.
Achievement motivation	Where one feels good about what one actually achieved.
Aptitude	How well one is suited to the job.
Diagnostic surveys	Psychological tools consist of two basic types – tests, which have tested validity; and questionnaires which, although useful for demonstrating points, cannot be justified as statistically valid instruments. Diagnostic surveys, as used in this book are a form of tool which makes no claim on validity but should help the reader understand something of his or her attitude in the areas of significance in the book.
Enabling	The ultimate delegation. Trusting others to do a job after having made sure that the objectives, ways and means are clear while maintaining a monitoring role.
Facilitation	Helping others to have the materials and skills to do a job while NOT actually helping with the job itself.
Feedback	Information given regularly to individuals or groups about performance.
Goals	Management jargon for the objectives set for workers.
Intervention	When groups or individuals have been unable to do work effectively, the outsider (tutor or manager) may decide, through his or her monitoring function, that things are not going as planned and step in (intervening) to reset or review.
Kaisen	A Japanese management philosophy of continuous improvement.
Learning organisation	A late 90s concept with as many definitions as management guru's. The underlying concept is that to survive in the 90s and beyond, organisations and individuals need to continually refresh their skills and knowledge.
Management by objectives (MBO)	A mechanistic management tool whereby employees develop, with their managers, encompassing goals which are SMART – Specific, Measurable, Agreed, Realistic and Timed. Management after the setting of the MBO goals is thus reduced to monitoring progress on these items.
Milestone reporting	A job is structured so that, as opposed to one final point of success or failure, many steps towards the goals are

	recognised. At these points (milestones) interim reports are formalised.
Monitoring	Watching and measuring and if necessary, intervening in a project to ensure that norms and quality are maintained.
Motivation	A combination of desire and commitment demonstrated by effort.
Performance	The product of ability and motivation. What people actually do.
Peter principle	Promotion beyond the individual's level of competence – the good salesperson may well be a terrible sales manager.
Positive reinforcement	Where good behaviour is praised.
Ocham's Razor	A basic form of problem-solving loved by Sherlock Holmes. 'Work on the most probable solutions first. When all these have been disposed of, the last, however improbable, is the solution'. That is, of course, assuming you have ALL the solutions listed and that the problem is solvable without redefinition.
Synergistic	The whole is greater than the parts.
Work study	A tool of 'scientific management' whereby jobs are reduced to elements. The elements are often allocated units of time and used for costing.

References

Atkinson, J. W. & Raynor, J. O. *Motivation and achievement*. Washington, D.C.: V. H. Winston, 1974.

Bradford, D. L. & Cohen, A. R. *Managing for excellence*. New York: John Wiley, 1984.

Cannon, Tom. *How to get ahead in business*. London: Virgin Books, 1993.

Colby, W. Motivation in motion. *Infosystems*, August 1985, 81-83.

Dalton, G., Lawrence, P. & Lorsch, J. *Organizational structure and design*. Homewood, Ill.: Irwin, 1970.

Financial Times, London, 19 April 1985.

Galloway, Alisdair. *Maintenance of hierarchy*, Doctoral thesis, University of Glasgow, 1990.

Gleick, J. *Chaos, making a new science.* William Heinmann Ltd, 1988.

Greene, C. N. The satisfaction-performance controversy. *Business Horizons*, 1972, 15, 31-41.

Greenberg, J. Approaching equity and avoiding inequity in groups and organizations. In J. Greenberg & R. L. Cohen (Eds.), *Equity and justice in social behavior*. New York: Academic Press, 1982.

Greenberg, J. & Ornstein, S. Motivation in organizations. In R. G. Geen, W. W. Beatty & R. M. Arkin (Eds.), *Human motivation: Physiological, behavioral, and social approaches*. Boston: Allyn and Bacon, 1984.

Guest, R.H. Of time and the foreman. *Personnel*, 1956, 32, 478-486.

Hackman, J. R. & Oldham, G. R. *Work redesign*. Reading, Mass.: Addison-Wesley, 1980.

Hammer, Michael & Champy, James. *Re-engineering the corporation*. London: Nicholas Brealey, 1993.

Hamner, W. C. Reinforcement theory and contingency management in organizational settings. In H. L. Tosi & W. C. Hamner (Eds.), *Organizational behavior and management: A contingency approach*. Chicago: St. Clair Press, 1974.

Handy, Charles. *The age of unreason*. London: Century Business, 1990.

Herriot, P. & Pemberton, C. *New Deals, The Revolution in Management Careers*. Wiley, 1995.

Hersey P. & Blanchard K. *The management of organisational behaviour*. Englewood Cliffs, N.J.: Prentice-Hall, 1982.

House, R. J. & Mitchell, T. R. Path-goal theory of leadership. *Journal of*

Contemporary Business, 1974, 3, 81-97.
Ivancevich, J. M. & McMahon, T. J. The effects of goal setting, external feedback and self-generated feedback on outcome variables: A field experiment. *Academy of Management Journal*, 1982, 23, 359-72.
Jay, A. *Management and Machiavelli, an inquiry into the politics of corporate life*. New York: Holt, Rinehart and Winston, 1967.
Jordan, Paul C. Effects of extrinsic rewards on intrinsic motivation: A field experiment. *Academy of Management Journal*, 1986, 27, 405-12.
Kellogg, M. S. *Putting management theories to work*. Englewood Cliffs, N.J.: Prentice-Hall, 1979.
Kerr, S. On the folly of rewarding A, while hoping for B. *Academy of Management Review*, 1975, 19, 769-783.
Kipnis, D. *The powerholders*. Chicago, Ill.: University of Chicago Press, 1976.
Kopelman, R. E. Job redesign and productivity: A review of evidence. *National Productivity Review*, Summer 1985, 237-255.
Latham, G. P., Cummings, L. L. & Mitchell, T. R. Behavioral strategies to improve productivity. *Organizational Dynamics*, 1981, 10, 5-23.
Latham, G., Erez, M. & Locke, E. Resolving scientific disputes by the joint design of crucial experiments by the antagonists: Application to the Erez-Latham disputes regarding participation in goal setting. *Journal of Applied Psychology*, 1988, 73, 753-772.
Latham, G. & Locke, E. Goal setting: a motivational technique that works. *Organizational Dynamics*, 1979, 8, 68-80.
Lawler, E. E., III. *Motivation in work organizations*. Belmont, Calif.: Brooks/Cole, 1973.
Lawler, E. E. *Pay and organizational effectiveness*. New York: McGraw-Hill, 1971.
LeDue, A. I., Jr. Motivation of programmers. *Data Base*, 1980, 3, 5.
Levering, R., Moskovitz, M. & Katz, M. *The 100 best companies to work for in America*. Reading, Mass.: Addison-Wesley, 1984.
Locke, E. A, Shaw, K., Saari, L. & Latham, G. Goal setting and task performance: 1969-1980. *Psychological Bulletin*, 1981, 90, 125-152.
Locke, E. & Latham, G. *Goal setting: A motivational technique that works*. Englewood Cliffs, N.J.: Prentice-Hall, 1984.
Luthans, F. & Kreitner, R. *Organizational behavior modification*. Glenview, Ill.: Scott Foresman, 1975.
Maier, N. R. F. *Psychology in industrial organizations* (4th ed.). New York: Houghton Mifflin, 1973.
Management Today, London, June 1988.
McGregor, D. *The human side of enterprise*. New York: McGraw-Hill, 1960.

Michener, H. A., Fleishman, J. A. & Vaske, J. J. A test of the bargaining theory of coalition formulation in four-person groups. *Journal of Personality and Social Psychology*, 1976, 34, 1114–1126.

Miner, J. B. The validity and usefulness of theories in an emerging organizational science. *Academy of Management Review*, 1984, 9, 296–306.

Nadler, D. E. & Lawler, E. E. Motivation: A diagnostic approach. In J. R. Hackman, E. E. Lawler & L. W. Porter (Eds.), *Perspective behavior in organizations*. New York: McGraw-Hill, 1977.

Nord, W. R. Some issues in the application of operant conditioning to the management of organizations. *Organization and Administrative Sciences*, 1975, 6, 55–62.

Peters, T. & Waterman, R. H. *In search of excellence*. London: HarperCollins, 1982.

Quick, T. L. *Person to person managing*. New York: St. Martin's Press, 1977.

Roethlisberger, F. J. & Dickson, W. J. *Management and the worker. An account of a research program conducted by the Western Electric Company (Hawthorne Works)*. Chicago, Cambridge Mass.: Harvard University Press, 1939.

Rossiter, R. *MBA Dissertation*. Bradford University, 1995.

Scott-Morgan, P. *Unwritten rules of the game*. McGraw Hill, 1994.

Semler, Ricardo. *Maverick*. London: Century, 1993.

Skinner, B. F. *Science and human behavior*. New York: Macmillan, 1953.

Snyder, M., Stephen, W. & Rosenfield, D. Attributional egotism. In J. Harvey, W. Ickes & R. Kidds (Eds.), *New directions in attributional research* (Vol. 2). Hillsdale, N.J.: Erlbaum, 1978.

Staw, B. M., McKechnie, P. & Puffer, S. The justification of organizational performance. *Administrative Science Quarterly*, 1983, 28, 582–600.

Stewart, Ian and Joines, Vann. *TA today*. Nottingham: Lifespace Publishing, 1987.

Syer, John. *Team spirit*. London: Simon & Schuster, 1986.

Thompson, D. W. *Managing people: Influencing behavior*. St. Louis: C.V. Mosby Co., 1978.

Wanous, J. P. *Organizational entry*. Reading, Mass.: Addison-Wesley, 1980.

White, M. & Trevor, M. *Under Japanese management: The experience of British workers*. PSI Heinemann, 1983.

Woods, Mike & Whitehead, Jackie. *Working alone*. London: Pitman, 1993.

Index